The
Eternal Purpose of God

The Eternal Purpose of God

Lance Lambert

Sovereign World

Sovereign World Ltd
PO Box 784
Ellel
Lancaster LA1 9DA
England

www.sovereignworld.com

ISBN: 978 1 85240 503 8

The publishers aim to produce books which will help to extend and build up
the Kingdom of God. We do not necessarily agree with every view expressed
by the authors, or with every interpretation of Scripture expressed. We expect
readers to make their own judgement in the light of their understanding of
God's Word and in an attitude of Christian love and fellowship.

Typeset by Hurix Systems Private Limited
Printed in Malta

CONTENTS

Foreword

The first time Lance came to Pip'n'Jay was in April 1969. He had
ministered at informal meetings in my home prior to that but
that Sunday was the first time he preached from our pulpit. He
preached on "Rent Veil, the Rolled Away Stone and the Open
Heaven" – referring to pictures he had seen in my home. It was,
needless to say, the beginning of a long relationship. Lance was
to return to Pip'n'Jay many times even after he had made his
home in Jerusalem. I know no one who can touch him as far as
Biblical teaching is concerned.

He is always clear, humorous and challenging. These three
qualities you will find in this book. When I first read it I reckoned I knew what the eternal purpose of God was and then
panicked to make sure that I had in fact got it right. I reckoned
that God's purpose was that this life was preparation for the
family membership in the world to come. I had not got the fact
in my brain that God wants to have a people fit to rule from the
heavenly Jerusalem. I should have got the 'reigning' bit right
because I had done a series of Bible studies on Paul's epistle to
the Romans. And in verse 17 of Chapter 5 it says there, "For if
by one man's offence death reigned by one; much more they
which receive abundance of grace and the gift of righteousness
shall reign in life by one, Jesus Christ". God's eternal purposes
for his church is that we should reign in life – we are definitely
above; see the end of Chapter 5 in this book.

I am glad to commend this book and trust that it will bring many into a more dynamic discipleship than they have previously experienced.

Reverend Canon Malcolm Widdecombe
St Phillips and St Jacobs
Bristol, August 2008

INTRODUCTION

This book has grown out of a series of studies which were given in many places, principally to begin with, in the early 1950s, in Halford House, Richmond, Surrey, in the United Kingdom, and then in Hong Kong, in the 1980s, and more latterly in Jerusalem in the 1990s. There have been many requests over the years to put it into writing. The Hong Kong series of messages were put into a small book, in both English and Chinese. Now I have been enabled, by the Lord, to take these different series and bring them together in this book.

There is no truth that is of greater importance than this matter of God's Eternal Purpose. Once a child of God, and a servant of God, begins to understand God's ultimate aim in time, and for the ages to come, our lives become more meaningful and significant. A new direction is given to us by the Spirit of God, through the Word of God. We understand in a new, deeper, and more relevant manner the longing expressed by the apostle Paul in his letter to the Colossians: "that in all things he [the Messiah Jesus] may have the preeminence" (1:18). We become as children of God, as servants of God, as workers in His vineyard, Christ centered.

This book was not produced as a result of mere academic study, but through the illumination which the Holy Spirit granted me, though totally unworthy, through His Word over the years of my life. I first began to see this matter when I was in my teens, and the Lord has given more light as year succeeded to year. The Lord used a number of His servants to sow the seeds in my heart of this book. One of those was our brother Watchman Nee of China; others were W. Graham Scroggie of Scotland, Brother Bakht Singh of India, and Theodore Austin-Sparks of the UK.

I trust the Lord that He will use this book to challenge, to encourage, to build up, and, where necessary, to correct. If there are faults, they are mine; and if there is essential and living truth, it is the Lord Jesus. In the course of these pages I repeat myself many times! I trust that such repetition will not be too tedious, but the means of clearer understanding.

I wish to acknowledge the many who have helped in the final production of it: Shirley Harrison of the USA, who transcribed a number of the original messages; Scott Miller of the USA and Nathan Gosling of the UK, who typed the manuscript; and David Carlsson of Sweden, Malcolm Norris of the USA, and Stephen Briggs of the UK, who looked after everything in the house and garden whilst the work was being done! I must also thank my publishers, especially Paul Stanier and his team, for their fellowship and endurance at all stages of its production.

May the Lord Jesus Himself use this book as a vehicle of light and grace to all who read it.

Lance Lambert
Jerusalem 2009

Chapter 1

ACCORDING TO HIS ETERNAL PURPOSE

The number of Christians who have an understanding of God's Eternal Purpose is few and the reason is simple. It is a truth that is normally relegated to the realm of theology, and is therefore considered by the majority of believers to be irrelevant to everyday life and experience. Yet the revelation of the purpose of God for the universe, for this planet, for mankind in general, and for the redeemed in particular is one of the major themes of the Bible. One wonders why the Holy Spirit has gone to such lengths to give us this revelation of God's heart and mind if it is impractical and basically irrelevant to everyday life.

In particular the Ephesian letter of the apostle Paul deals with this whole question of God's Eternal Purpose. It is generally recognized by believing theologians and Bible teachers to be the high-water mark of divine revelation in the New Testament. So tremendous is this revelation that the phrases and words seem to flow out of the apostle like a great river, overwhelming the mind. It is an illustration of what he himself described as an opened door of utterance or articulation to communicate the mystery of the gospel and the mystery of Christ (see Ephesians 6:19; Colossians 4:3). Still to this day the breadth and the length, the height and the depth of the revelation which the Holy Spirit communicated through this man of God overpower us: it brings us face to face with the infinity of God.

Even with the most superficial reading of the Ephesian letter, it becomes apparent that it concerns divine purpose and the will of God from eternity to eternity. The word "purpose" and the phrase "the will of God" lie at the heart of what Paul, by the Holy Spirit, is communicating. Furthermore, that purpose and will of God are always declared to be centered in the person of the Lord Jesus, and those whom He saves and joins to Himself. The phrase which the Holy Spirit empowered the apostle Paul to use in writing this letter is pregnant with significance and meaning: "according to the eternal purpose which [God] purposed in Christ Jesus our Lord" (Ephesians 3:11, NASB "carried out"). If we believe in the divine authority and inspiration of the Word of God, this phrase becomes a window into the heart and the mind of God.

Paul had already declared in the first chapter that God was "making known unto us the mystery of his will, according to his good pleasure which he purposed in him . . . to sum up all things in Christ." He went on to write that those who were saved by the grace of God were being "made a heritage . . . according to the purpose of him who worketh all things after the counsel of his will" (Ephesians 1:9, 11).

It is clear that this matter of God's Eternal Purpose is of vital importance to the Church of God, to the work of God, and to the child of God. Is it any wonder that Satan has made it one of his supreme strategies to keep the redeemed ignorant of this purpose? It is sad that this strategy has been so successful, for the ignorance of it is widespread.

Indeed, for many Christian believers, the concept of the Christian life is more of a routine than a day-to-day experience of His life and power. The commonly held idea is that when we have been converted, we should pray at least once a day; we should also read the Bible once a day; we should attend church at least once a week; and if we are very spiritual and devoted,

we should seek to win others to Christ. Then at some point, we
will go to be forever with the Lord, somewhere in the atmosphere. There in a kind of glorified night gown, and with harp in
hand, we will be part of an eternal Hallelujah choir!

Is it any wonder that the sophisticated world around us ridi-
cules such a concept! Is this truly the gospel? Did the Father, at
enormous cost, send the Son to be the Savior of the world for
merely this? Has the Lord Jesus endured the cross, taking upon
Himself all the iniquity and sin of the world, tasting death for
every man, with so limited a goal in view? Apart from any other
consideration, what kind of character has the God who would
be satisfied for an endless eternity with an endless choir singing
His endless praises!

In stating this I do not for a moment wish to ridicule what
are, after all, biblical figures of speech. The Word of God does
speak of "harps" and "white garments" and unbelievable worship and praise! It is the fact that those figures of speech are
often not understood that is so serious. My intention is not to
diminish the value of prayer, or Bible study, or the assembling
of ourselves together with other believers, or evangelism; and it
is certainly not my aim to devalue genuine worship in spirit and
in truth. Nevertheless, to be ignorant of God's Eternal Purpose,
when you have a Bible in your hands, is folly of the first order!
Such ignorance is not bliss, but foolishness. If God *has* an eternal
purpose and has saved us according to that purpose, and has
given us the revelation of it in His Word, and sent the Holy
Spirit to enlighten us and to bring revelation and illumination
to us, *it is surely incumbent upon the child of God to seek Him for
understanding of that purpose*. It is, after all, the birthright of every
true child of God to have such enlightenment.

Why did God create this universe and this earth, which at
our present extent of knowledge is unique? What was His aim
and goal in its creation? Why did He create mankind? And when
man fell short of His glory through sin, why did He persevere
and provide salvation? Is that salvation an end in itself, or is it

a means to an end, with everything provided within it to reach the final goal? And how can I be involved in the fulfillment of that purpose? If any single one of the readers of this book should become clearer on these issues, it would make its writing worthwhile!

Many Christians believe that God's Eternal Purpose *is* salvation and, in a very real sense, that is true. No one can be involved in the fulfillment of that purpose without a personal experience of His salvation. God, however, had an original purpose before man fell, and His salvation is the glorious and powerful means to return us to it, and to involve us in its fulfillment. It is entirely noteworthy that the Bible ends with a wedding: the marriage of the Lamb and the wife of the Lamb. To some, it may seem a strange way for the Word of God to reach its conclusion. That wedding, in one sense, is the end of one whole long and painful phase in divine history: the purpose of God has reached its fulfillment in it. However, it is also the beginning of a new, glorious and eternal phase: the outworking of that fulfillment.

"I make all things new"

What does it mean when the Lord says in the last chapters of the Bible,

> And I saw the holy city, new Jerusalem, coming down out of heaven from God, made ready as a bride adorned for her husband. And I heard a great voice out of the throne saying, Behold, the tabernacle of God is with men, and he shall dwell with them, and they shall be his peoples, and God himself shall be with them, and be their God: and he shall wipe away every tear from their eyes; and death shall be no more; neither shall there be mourning, nor crying, nor pain, any more: the first things are passed away. And he that sitteth on the throne said, Behold, I make all things new.
>
> (Revelation 21:2–5)

If this world, so sin-marred and defaced, still reveals His power, His beauty, and His intelligence, even in its fallen state, what will it be when the former things have passed away and He makes all things new?

It is abundantly clear that the Lord intends to go on to even more wonderful works. It was the impact of this truth which caused the apostle Paul to write those marvelous words:

> but we speak God's wisdom in a mystery, the hidden wisdom which God predestined before the ages to our glory; the wisdom which none of the rulers of this age has understood; for if they had understood it, they would not have crucified the Lord of glory; but just as it is written, "Things which eye has not seen and ear has not heard, and which have not entered the heart of man, all that God has prepared for those who love Him." For to us God revealed them through the Spirit . . .
>
> (1 Corinthians 2:7–10 NASB)

The amazing beauty of this planet, its complex and intricate design, even in its fallen and disfigured state, causes us to worship the Creator. It is, however, a paralyzed creation! Concerning this, the apostle Paul declares,

> For I consider that the sufferings of this present time are not worthy to be compared with the glory that is to be revealed to us. For the anxious longing of the creation waits eagerly for the revealing of the sons of God. For the creation was subjected to futility, not of its own will, but because of Him who subjected it, in hope that the creation itself also will be set free from its slavery to corruption into the freedom of the glory of the children of God. For we know that the whole creation groans and suffers the pains of childbirth together until now.
>
> (Romans 8:18–22 NASB)

By any reckoning, this is an extraordinary revelation. Through it we understand that this whole natural creation is in slavery to corruption, trapped within an endless cycle of futility and groaning with the labor pains of childbirth. What will it be, and what will it become, when it is released into "the freedom of the glory of the children of God"? The dramatic manner in which the Word of God describes it, is in itself significant. Labor pains normally lead to birth!

God has not exhausted His creative genius, having nothing more to produce or to create in the future! He has certainly not retired, with no more to do than to vegetate! He is awaiting the appointed date of that wedding, when He will begin to fulfill what He originally intended.

The need to walk wisely

Toward the end of the Ephesian letter, Paul writes:

> Look therefore carefully how ye walk, not as unwise, but as wise; redeeming the time, because the days are evil. Wherefore be ye not foolish, but understand what the will of the Lord is.
>
> (5:15–17)

Carefully note the "therefore" and the "wherefore." Paul is connecting what he is now writing with the revelation in this letter of God's Eternal Purpose. He speaks of walking not as unwise but as wise. In the Word of God, "walking" always implies something practical and relevant, the practical outworking of spiritual truth. Children of God are to walk in the light of the revelation of God's purpose. Paul declares that we need to be "wise walkers"! Only those who in evil days walk wisely *will redeem the time* in which they live.

Paul continues: "wherefore, be ye not foolish, but understand what the will of the Lord is." The reference here to the will of God is generally understood as relating to our personal and family needs: What should I do? What path should I take? What career should I pursue? What college should I choose? Where should I live? Whom should I marry? What community of believers should I join? All of these matters are vital and important, and in facing them we obviously need to know the will of God. However, to have an understanding of God's overall and eternal purpose is to put all of these issues into a proper perspective. In fact, more often than not, a lot of our queries would be answered by such an understanding. The fact that Paul uses the words "wise" and "unwise," and "foolish" emphasizes this. Therefore it seems clear to me that the apostle is speaking of God's Eternal Purpose when he says, "be ye not foolish, but understand what the will of the Lord is." With such an understanding of His Eternal Purpose, we are to *walk*.

"A spirit of wisdom and revelation in the knowledge of Christ"

We should also note Paul's prayer burden which he expressed in the early part of this letter:

> For this cause I also . . . cease not to give thanks for you, making mention of you in my prayers; that the God of our Lord Jesus Christ, the Father of glory, may give unto you a spirit of wisdom and revelation in the knowledge of him; having the eyes of your heart enlightened, that ye may know what is the hope of his calling, what the riches of the glory of his inheritance in the saints, and what the exceeding greatness of his power to us-ward who believe . . .
>
> (Ephesians 1:15–19)

The difference between wisdom and knowledge

The apostle's words reveal a burden for the believers at Ephesus. He was deeply concerned that the revelation of God's Eternal

Purpose could become mere head knowledge, mere theology, or simply essential divine truth with no practical outworking or experience. Apparently, he was so troubled by this possibility that he felt he should let the believers know the burden that was driving him to pray for them. We can only praise the Lord that he expressed this concern, for it corrects a mentality amongst some Christian believers, and even servants of the Lord, that we can study doctrine academically without the need of spiritual illumination and understanding.

This has very great and vital importance for us in the twenty-first century. The ignorance today of God's Eternal Purpose is largely due to the fact that we do not see any need to seek the Lord for understanding of it. Paul speaks of a "spirit of wisdom and revelation in the knowledge of the Lord Jesus" being granted to us. Wisdom is more than knowledge. Knowledge is to do with facts; wisdom is to do with how to handle those facts.

Years ago when I lived in Richmond, Surrey, England, outside of my study in Halford House was a magnificent fuchsia standard tree. Every year it was loaded with bloom. On one particular year, the buds all developed and then suddenly fell off. The bush then produced more bloom, and again the same thing happened. Within the fellowship were two much revered botanists, both of them working at the Herbarium in the famous Kew Gardens; and I asked them for their help. Interestingly, they both went through the same procedure: they plucked a leaf, held it up to the light, scratched its trunk, and sought to expose a root. Both of them gave me a run-down of the history of this species of fuchsia, which was almost encyclopedic, and explained the various possible diseases from which it could be suffering. When, however, I asked what I should do, both of them were stumped. One of them even said, "Well, it will either live or die!"

Adjacent to Halford House was a market garden run by Dan Archer, a Derbyshire man and a gardener of no small character! In fact, he was the personality upon which was based the famous long-running BBC series called *The Archers*. I asked Dan Archer to come down and have a look at the fuchsia, which he did. He went through much the same procedure as the botanists and then said, "This bush needs a daily tablespoon of Epsom salts for two weeks." Now these salts are a purgative, used for human "inner cleanliness"! Naturally, I thought he was joking! No, he said, he was not joking, for that was what the bush needed. I felt that I could not bear the whole fellowship knowing that I was dosing the fuchsia bush with Epsom salts, so I asked the sister in charge of the house if she would do it, and she fulfilled the required duty! The fuchsia recovered literally within a month, and once again gave everyone great pleasure. Here we see the difference between knowledge and wisdom. Knowledge is to do with facts; wisdom is how to handle the facts: what to do with them.

When Paul speaks of a spirit of wisdom and revelation in the knowledge of Christ, he is not speaking of head knowledge. He is speaking of experiencing Him in an ever deeper and fuller way, life changing in its impact. For this we need both divine wisdom and divine revelation. This revelation is not extra to the Word of God, but it is the Holy Spirit's illumination of that Word. In fact, the Lord Jesus promised,

> Howbeit when he, the Spirit of truth, is come, he shall guide you into all the truth . . . He shall glorify me: for he shall take of mine, and shall declare it unto you.
>
> (John 16:13–14)

Without the Holy Spirit, we have only a mentally received knowledge of the truth. We have no living experience of it: and our lives and our beings are left unaffected and unchanged. When, however, the Holy Spirit takes the truth as it is in the Lord Jesus and "declares it" to us, the Word of Christ dwells in us; we receive an implanted word (see Colossians 3:16; James 1:21).

For those who read these words and feel somehow that they have no understanding of God's Eternal Purpose but desire to have such an understanding, the words of the Lord Jesus are clear:

> Ask, and it shall be given you; seek, and ye shall find; knock, and it shall be opened unto you: for every one that asketh receiveth; and he that seeketh findeth; and to him that knocketh it shall be opened.
>
> (Matthew 7:7–8)

He also said,

> I thank thee, O Father, Lord of heaven and earth, that thou didst hide these things from the wise and understanding, and didst reveal them unto babes . . . Take my yoke upon you, and learn of me; for I am meek and lowly in heart: and ye shall find rest unto your souls.
>
> (Matthew 11:25, 29)

A little infant, a babe, knows nothing. It is hard for adults, especially intelligent ones, to humble themselves and become as little children; but there is no alternative. The Lord stated it simply: "Take my yoke upon you, and learn of me." It is a double yoke, and when we humble ourselves enough to accept that yoke, we discover Him beside us, and we learn of Him. Could there be, in this universe, anything more wonderful than to be yoked with the Lord Jesus, and to learn of Him through all the up and down experiences of everyday life?

Chapter 2

VISION, FAITH, AND OBEDIENCE

In the last chapter, I wrote of the necessity of having the eyes of the heart enlightened. The Word of God, throughout its sixty-six books, places tremendous emphasis upon the need to "see." Many times the observation is made, "they have eyes, but see not." Indeed, the Lord Jesus Himself said:

> Therefore, speak I to them in parables; because seeing they see not, and hearing they hear not, neither do they understand.
>
> (Matthew 13:13)

Even more striking is the fact that He spoke to the church in Laodicea, to born-again believers, and said:

> Because thou sayest, I am rich, and have gotten riches, and have need of nothing; and knowest not that thou art the wretched one and miserable and poor and blind and naked: I counsel thee to buy of me . . . eyesalve to anoint thine eyes, that thou mayest see.
>
> (Revelation 3:17–19)

Is it possible for a child of God, saved by the grace of God and born of the Spirit of God, to be blind? Evidently so! It is clearly a possibility to suffer delusion, believing that one is rich and has need of nothing, whereas the Lord's estimate is altogether different. He speaks of His church, and of His child, as "the wretched one and miserable and poor and blind and naked." In the enormous discrepancy between the self-estimate of this church or the individual believers in it and the Lord's estimate of the true condition of both, we see the absolute necessity of vision.

What do we mean by the "eyes of the heart"? It is recorded of Moses that "he endured, as seeing him who is invisible" (Hebrews 11:27). How can anyone see One who is "invisible"? We should carefully note that with Moses this was not a one-off "vision." He "endured" as seeing Him who is invisible. In other words, it was an ongoing experience. David had the same kind of experience when he declares:

I have set the Lord always before me:

Because he is at my right hand, I shall not be moved.

(Psalm 16:8)

By a new birth, God has constituted the child of God with a spiritual ability to behold the Lord. It is not physical, but spiritual. The writer of the Hebrew letter speaks of "looking unto Jesus, the author and finisher of our faith" (12:2). The apostle Paul likewise writes:

But we all with unveiled face, beholding as in a mirror the glory of the Lord, are being transformed into the same image from glory to glory, just as from the Lord, the Spirit . . . For God, who said, "Light shall shine out of darkness," is the One who has shone in our hearts to give the Light of the knowledge of the glory of God in the face of Christ.

(2 Corinthians 3:18; 4:6 NASB)

This is not in any way to devalue genuine physical visions of the Lord, both in the Old Testament period and in the New, and in the history of the true Church of God. *Spiritual* sight, however, is basic and essential to the well-being of the child of God.

The Word of God states that:

Where there is no vision, the people cast off restraint.

(Proverbs 29:18)

We have the same Hebrew word in 1 Samuel 3:1:

And the word of the Lord was rare [mg] in those days; there was no frequent vision.

This word, translated in English by "vision," comes from a root word in Hebrew meaning "to behold." Whilst this word can refer to ecstatic visions, it also has the meaning of prophetic vision, or prophetic understanding. Hence the NASB marginal rendering, "Where there is no revelation . . . " It is also important to note that the Hebrew word translated in the KJV "perish" and in the ASV "cast off restraint," simply means "to unbind," "to let go," "to go to pieces," and thus "to perish." Wherever there is vision, a prophetic understanding given by the Holy Spirit, a living revelation of the heart and mind of God, the Eternal Purpose of God touches the earth; and some stage in its fulfillment is reached. This has been true of the whole history of the Old Testament period, of the New Testament period, and throughout the history of the Church. Likewise, whenever there has been no prophetic understanding of the heart and mind of God, a spiritual paralysis has developed, with all its consequences: disorder, lack of direction, confusion, and spiritual death.

Abraham the father of all who believe

One of those great turning points in history was reached with Abraham. Speaking before the Sanhedrin, Stephen recalls:

The God of glory appeared unto our father Abraham, when he was in Mesopotamia, before he dwelt in Haran, and said unto

him, Get thee out of thy land, and from thy kindred, and come
into the land which I shall show thee.

(Acts 7:2–3)

The writer of the Hebrew letter records:

By faith Abraham, when he was called, obeyed to go out
unto a place which he was to receive for an inheritance;
and he went out, not knowing whither he went. By faith he
became a sojourner in the land of promise, as in a land not his
own . . . for he looked for the city which hath the foundations,
whose builder and maker is God.

(11:8–10)

We should note that this vision of the God of glory changed
Abraham's whole life. It was not merely an ecstatic vision which
left him the same. Everything changed. According to Jewish tradition, Abraham came from one of the great aristocratic and
ruling families of Ur of the Chaldees. The wealth of the family came from idol making, and Abraham was one of the top
salesmen. When the God of glory appeared to Abraham, he
was blown into another dimension. On no single level of his
life were things ever the same. From being a city dweller, he
became a pilgrim, a transient. From being a wealthy landowner,
he became a landless nomad. From being a pagan and producer
of idols in gold, in silver, in wood, and in stone, he became the
worshiper of the living and invisible God, and, at the same time,
a dealer in sheep and goats, in camels and donkeys! What was it
that changed him?

When the one true and living God, the Creator of all things
with neither beginning nor end, appeared to Abraham, he never
worshiped an idol again, nor spirits in mountains, or in rocks,
or in rivers; he became a true worshiper. He became a believer
in the living God. This gift of faith was so real and so powerful,
so foundational to his whole life, that he came to be called "the

father of all who believe." Indeed, Paul writes that we, who are the recipients of the same living faith, are blessed with "believing Abraham" (Galatians 3:9 JND). Even when Abraham failed, as with Pharaoh, and Abimelech, and over Ishmael, he never returned to idol worship. Something had gripped Abraham, and it never left him. In the God of glory, he saw salvation, deliverance, and a new beginning, with a new life and a new destiny.

It is remarkable that the Lord Jesus declared:

> Your father Abraham rejoiced to see my day; and he saw it, and was glad.
>
> (John 8:56)

The vision Abraham had of God was a prophetic revelation. In one sense, he saw the whole of human history centered in the coming and the work of the Messiah Jesus. In this sense, he was clearer than many Christians today! The Lord had said to Abraham:

> I will make of thee a great nation . . . and in thee shall all the families of the earth be blessed.
>
> (Genesis 12:2–3)

Abraham understood that his life and his seed, through Isaac, were somehow bound up with both the salvation of Israel and the salvation of the Gentiles, and he saw that salvation centered in the Messiah Jesus. Daniel, much later in history, was also to understand that his life and ministry were similarly bound up with the coming of the Messiah and His finished work (see Daniel 9). The Lord Jesus said that Abraham rejoiced to see His day, emphasizing that fact by adding: "he saw it, and was glad." It was not some fleeting and flimsy idea that Abraham had, that somehow, in the distant future, a Messiah would come: it was something so substantial and real that Abraham worshiped and rejoiced.

When Abraham saw the God of glory, in some manner he saw the city of glory. By the vision he had, and the understanding given through it, he saw the city of God as somehow the key to world history. In fact, he saw the Messiah and the Bride of the Messiah, the wife of the Lamb. He had left no mean city when he left Ur of the Chaldees. So great was the vision he received that he never returned to it, not even as a tourist! That great city, with all its sophistication and power, left him cold. He discerned that it did not have eternal foundations. Instead, he sought for that city which has those foundations, the heavenly Jerusalem. In the whole of Abraham's life, as far as we know, he never lived in Jerusalem for even a short period; yet his life was bounded by its divine significance and meaning. We could say that the Jerusalem which is above was the mother of Abraham (see Galatians 4:26).

In seeing the God of glory, Abraham saw the city of God's glory, and understood God's Eternal Purpose. For him, the history and destiny of the world was divided into two cities: on the one hand, Babylon or Babel, of which spiritually Ur was part, and, on the other hand, Jerusalem. Every human being has his birth registration in one or the other. So great is the grace of God that you can be born in the former and re-registered by a new birth in the latter (see Psalm 87). Abraham was spoilt for anything less than God's best. In that vision of the God of glory, Abraham heard the divine call and by faith obeyed, and "went out, not knowing whither he went." The living faith with which God had gifted him, flung him into the arms of God. It was a journey which was to end in eternal glory.

The principle of spiritual vision

This principle of spiritual vision, and the life-changing understanding that it brings, is everywhere in the Bible. Whether it is Jacob who, fearful and alone, devastated by the revelation of his own hopeless self-life, would not let the Lord go, crying "Bless me," and who described that experience at Jabbok as "the face of God," changing him from Jacob the twister into Israel the prince with God. Or whether it is Moses and the revelation of the Being and the Character of God which he received when God appeared to him in a thorn bush in the desert. The I AM was in that thorn bush: He was the fire, Moses was the dead bush; He was the fire, and Israel was the dead bush. Or whether it is Isaiah, when the Lord gave him a vision of Himself, high and lifted up, His train filling the temple. Out of that vision, and the understanding of it, flowed one of the richest prophetic ministries in the Word of God. In these lives, and many more, this principle of spiritual vision is underlined.

The example of Paul

Another great turning point in history was the conversion of the apostle Paul. In his testimony before King Agrippa, Paul said:

> at midday, O king, I saw on the way a light from heaven, above the brightness of the sun, shining round about me and them that journeyed with me. And when we were all fallen to the earth, I heard a voice saying unto me in the Hebrew language, Saul, Saul, why persecutest thou me? It is hard for thee to kick against the goad. And I said, Who art thou, Lord? And the Lord said, I am Jesus whom thou persecutest . . . Wherefore, O king Agrippa, I was not disobedient unto the heavenly vision . . .
>
> (Acts 26:13–15, 19)

That this was what has been described as an "ecstatic" vision is clear. What is also as clear is the fact that out of this vision came a revelation of the heart and mind of God. For Paul, this vision was the seedbed of his entire ministry, which he described as preaching "the unsearchable riches of Christ"! Whether he understood it immediately or progressively in the years that followed, its source was in that vision.

When the Lord confronted Saul of Tarsus, He did not say: "Why are you persecuting My followers, the ones I am saving?" He said, "Why are you persecuting *Me?*" and emphasized it even more when He went on to say, "I am Jesus, whom you are persecuting." Paul could have said, "I am not persecuting You; I am persecuting Your followers." It was out of this vision that Paul's whole understanding of the church as the body of Christ came (see, for example, Colossians 1:18; Ephesians 1:22–23; Ephesians 4:15–16; 1 Corinthians 12:12, etc.). He understood the essential unity of the Lord Jesus with those whom He saves.

Indeed, the apostle Paul saw the whole purpose of God centered in the Lord Jesus. The phrase which most adequately describes his ministry is "in Christ." He understood that our whole salvation was in Christ; all the blessings were in Him; all the supply of our needs was in Him; all the fullness of God was in Him, and we are complete in Him (see, for example, 2 Timothy 2:10; Ephesians 1:3; Philippians 4:19; Colossians 2:9–10). He saw everything of God as being in Christ, and nothing outside of Him. He would have understood the Gospel of John very clearly in this light.

> In the beginning was the Word, and the Word was with God, and the Word was God . . . And the Word became flesh, and dwelt among us (and we beheld his glory, glory as of the only begotten of the Father), full of grace and truth . . . No man hath seen God at any time; the only begotten Son, who is in the bosom of the Father, he hath declared him. (John 1:1, 14, 18)
> I am the bread of life . . . (6:35)
> I am the light of the world . . . (8:12)
> I am the door of the sheep. (10:7)
> I am the good shepherd . . . (10:11)
> I am the resurrection and the life . . . (11:25)
> I am the way, and the truth, and the life . . . (14:6)
> I am the true vine . . . (15:1)
> Before Abraham was born, I am. (8:58)

It is all Christ!

When the apostle gave his testimony before King Agrippa, he summed up all he had to say by stating: "wherefore, O King Agrippa, I was not disobedient unto the heavenly vision." Faith and obedience are living twins, never to be divided. Obedience is, in fact, the real and the tangible evidence of living faith.

"The hope of His calling"

It is interesting to note that the writer of the Hebrew letter describes the vision that Abraham had as being something to do with "calling." In other words, when the God of glory appeared to Abraham, He *called* him to begin the journey that would lead him to glory. Certainly with the apostle Paul, this matter of divine calling was all-important. For instance, he says: "I . . . beseech you to walk worthily of the calling wherewith ye were called." And, a few sentences later: "even as also ye were called in one hope of your calling" (Ephesians 4:1, 4). Writing to Timothy, he speaks of the God: "who saved us, and called us with a holy calling" (2 Timothy 1:9). I have already written about the prayer burden that Paul had for the Ephesian believers, when he prayed that God would give them a spirit of wisdom and revelation in the knowledge of Christ, having the eyes of their heart enlightened that they would know what was "the hope of His calling . . . "

Is this divine calling only to do with salvation, or does it entail something more? Why is there such an emphasis on the *hope* of one's calling? In the apostle's Roman letter, he wrote:

> We know that to them that love God all things work together for good, even to them that are called according to his purpose . . . whom he foreordained, them he also called: and whom he called, them he also justified: and whom he justified, them he also glorified.
>
> (8:28, 30)

This quotation would seem to suggest that it is concerned only with salvation.

No human being can be called of God without first having been saved by His grace. We should note that our salvation is a full and complete salvation; there is nothing to be added, and there is nothing to be subtracted: it is the *finished* work of the Lord Jesus. No human being can reach the divine goal or purpose without that salvation. Within it, all the grace of God, and all the power of the Holy Spirit, is available to the weakest and most hopeless sinner to enable them to reach God's end. *Nevertheless, our salvation is the means to the end, and not the end.*

We must take serious note of the use of the word "hope." It is the *hope* of our calling. In what is the most remarkable testimony in the Bible, the apostle Paul declares:

> Brethren, I count not myself yet to have laid hold: but one thing I do, forgetting the things which are behind, and stretching forward to the things which are before, I press on toward the goal unto the prize of the high calling of God in Christ Jesus.
>
> (Philippians 3:13–14)

If the great apostle could declare that *he did not count himself yet to have laid hold*, where does that leave you and me? This "high calling of God" is *in* the Messiah Jesus! There is no divine calling apart from Him: it is only in relation to Him. In Christ Jesus, there is a high calling of God, a goal to be reached, and a prize to be won! We need the Holy Spirit to come upon us with the same devoted determination to win that prize.

Chapter 3

THE BEGINNING AND THE
END OF THE BIBLE

The writer of the Hebrew letter tells us that "the word of God is living, and active, and sharper than any two-edged sword, and piercing even to the dividing of soul and spirit . . . " (4:12). This has certainly been my experience. I was brought up to understand that the Bible was full of legends, myths, inaccuracies, and exaggerations. Over a lifetime of studying the Word of God, I have failed to find these legends and inaccuracies! Instead, I have discovered that the Bible is unique. No word of Shakespeare or Goethe or Dickens has ever brought a human being to a new birth, nor delivered an alcoholic or a drug addict from his or her addiction. Yet, this Word of God, anywhere between 4,000 and 2,000 years old, is as alive, as active and as creative as when it was first given. It still lays open the thoughts and intents of the heart.

It does not matter in which way we approach the Bible, it is remarkable. Sixty-six books with one theme, spanning thousands of years, written through men inspired by the Holy Spirit at different points in time, and coming from different backgrounds and culture: from Job to Paul, from Abraham to John. *The basic theme is the Messiah, the Lord Jesus.*

The apostle Paul used a phrase which has been already quoted in the first chapter: "according to the eternal purpose which [God] purposed in Christ Jesus our Lord." The KJV, ERV and ASV all translate it "purposed in Christ." The RSV translates it "realized in Christ." The NASB "carried out in Christ." From this we clearly understand that God's Eternal Purpose was secured *only* in Christ. God purposed and realized that purpose, securing it, in and through Him.

From this we learn our first vital and all-important lesson concerning God's Eternal Purpose. It is wholly centered in the person of the Lord Jesus. The only way you and I can be introduced to this purpose of God, and involved in it, is through the Lord Jesus. Apart from Him, God has no eternal purpose. We should also note that this is not in the plural. It is not "purposes." When it comes to the eternal, God has only one purpose; and that purpose is centered in the Lord Jesus.

We see a three-fold cord that begins in Genesis and ends in Revelation. It consists of the Redeemer, the Work of Redemption, and the Redeemed. This three-fold cord is indivisible. Wherever we turn in the Word of God, we are confronted by it. This redemption, which cost the Redeemer everything, brings the redeemed back into the Eternal Purpose of God (see chart ii, also compare chart iv).

We also need to recognize another fact about the Bible. We can divide the Bible into three parts: origins; processes; and issues or outcome. In the book of Genesis, we have origins, the source of everything. In the book of Revelation, we have the issues or outcome: we see that origin determines destiny. From the book of Exodus to the letter of Jude, we have the processes (see chart iii). Thus, the Bible is not some jumble of sixty-six books, but is an amazing unity, which, once recognized, is stunning in its impact. It becomes clear that it is truly the *Word of God*.

An amazing correspondence

Even more remarkable is the correspondence between the first three chapters of Genesis and the last three chapters of Revelation (see chart iii). The minute and incredible correspondence between these chapters at the beginning and the end of the Bible cannot be coincidence. It reveals a design, and therefore a Designer! God, by His Spirit, is saying something! It is a striking fact that if we take the first two chapters of Genesis and the last two chapters of Revelation, we have the beginning and the end of a purpose: that divine purpose would have been fulfilled without Satan, without sin, and without the Fall. Only in the third chapter of Genesis do we have the record of the entrance of Satan and the fall of man, and only in the twentieth chapter of Revelation do we have the end of Satan and of sin. When this matter first dawned on me, in my late teens, it changed my life. I suddenly saw that something so detailed could only have been planned. It brought me into an understanding of God's Eternal Purpose, and saved me, by His grace, from the shallow and the superficial.

The correspondence between the beginning and the end of the Bible is even more astonishing when one realizes that the Apocalypse, or the book of Revelation, did not originally occupy the last place in the canon of the New Testament. For quite a number of years, it was attached either to the Gospel of John and his three letters, or to the four gospels, or to the book of Acts. Only in the beginning of the fourth century did it occupy the final position in the sixty-six books of the Bible.

In the first three chapters of Genesis, we have the creation of heaven and earth; in the last three chapters of Revelation, there is a new heaven and a new earth, wherein dwells righteousness. In the first three chapters, paradise is lost; in the last three chapters, paradise is regained. In the first three chapters, Satan enters; in the last three chapters, Satan is cast out forever. In the first three chapters, earth is cursed; in the last three chapters, "no curse anymore." In the first three chapters, there are two human beings – Adam and Eve; in the last three chapters, they have become a redeemed people that no man can number. In the first three chapters, there is a garden; in the last three chapters, there is a city. Interestingly, the city is a garden city, but it is a city. So first there is a garden, and in the last three chapters, as it were, the garden has become a city. In the first three chapters, there is the tree of life in the midst of the garden; in the last three chapters, there is the tree of life in the midst of the city. In the first three chapters, there is a river whose source is in the garden, and which becomes four great rivers that water the earth; in the last three chapters, we have the river of life, which proceeds out of the throne of God, out of the midst of the city. In the first three chapters, God walks in the midst of the garden, visiting once a day apparently to fellowship with Adam and Eve; in the last three chapters, God is "at home." He dwells forever in the midst of His city.

In the first three chapters, there is an earthly marriage – Adam and Eve. In Genesis chapter two, we are told the whole story of marriage and its institution; in the last three chapters, there is a heavenly marriage between the Lamb and the wife of the Lamb.

An earthly union – Adam and Eve: earthly marriage

Let us examine more fully this particular correspondence. In Genesis chapter one, we have the facts:

> God created man in his own image, in the image of God created he him; male and female created he them.
>
> (Genesis 1:27)

The fact is simply stated: man is male and female, i.e. two kinds of man make up the whole! They cannot subsist without each other (see 1 Corinthians 11:11, 12). In Genesis 2:18–25, we have the full account of the creation of man and woman. The manner in which the Holy Spirit introduces this account is significant. It begins with the words:

> And the Lord God said, It is not good that the man should be alone; I will make him a help meet for him.

The word "help meet" is interesting. The Hebrew means there was no one who "answered" to him or "corresponded" to him. The Holy Spirit then records that the Lord brought all the animals and birds before Adam for him to name them.

I had never read the Bible when I was twelve years of age, and when I first read it, I could not understand why the Lord did not Himself name the animals, since He had created them and therefore understood them. Now I understand: Adam did not realize that he was incomplete, and the Lord, in His own amazing way, was seeking to bring out that essential inner loneliness and incompleteness, which was in Adam. In other words, He was testing Adam as to whether Adam could settle down with one of these creatures. It was as if the Lord was saying, "Can you live with this?" And Adam said, "I will call this an elephant," and it went on its way; and so with the hippopotamus, and the giraffe, and the lion, and all the others. Even when he named the orang-utan, which in Bahasa Malay means "man of the forest," and which we are told is the nearest of all creatures to the human being, Adam named it and sent it on its way. The fact that the story of the naming of the animals ends with the same statement with which it began, "but for man there was not found a help meet for him," means that the Lord was underlining this matter of Adam's incompleteness.

> And the Lord God caused a deep sleep to fall upon the man, and he slept; and he took one of his ribs, and closed up the flesh instead thereof: and the rib, which the Lord God had taken from the man, made he a woman, and brought her unto the man. And the man said, This is now bone of my bones, and flesh of my flesh: she shall be called Woman, because she was taken out of Man.
>
> (Genesis 2:21–23)

When Adam first saw Eve, he saw himself. In the Hebrew, "man" is *ish*, and "woman" is *ishah*. The Word of God then records,

> Therefore shall a man leave his father and his mother, and shall cleave unto his wife: and they shall be one flesh.

Thousands of years later, by the Holy Spirit the apostle Paul states, "this mystery is great: but I speak in regard of Christ and of the church" (Ephesians 5:32).

A spiritual union – Christ and His Bride: eternal marriage

When the Lord Jesus, as the Second Man, the New Man, and the Last Adam, was crucified, in the darkest part of those hours He cried out, "My God, my God, why hast thou forsaken me?" (Mark 15:34). At the end of those three terrible but glorious hours, with a strong voice He shouted but one word, whether he used Hebrew, or Aramaic, or as recorded in Greek: "Finished." It means "accomplished, completed, or fulfilled". In that moment, the veil in the temple was torn in two from top to bottom, signifying the winning of an eternal salvation, and the making and the sealing by God of a new and eternal covenant with man. In those six hours, the Messiah Jesus had accomplished our salvation.

John, the most meditative and reflective of the twelve apostles, and probably the one with the deepest vision other than the apostle Paul, records that soldiers came to see if Jesus was dead: and one of them pierced His side with a spear, and out of it came blood and water. Then John said, as if this fact was of the utmost importance:

> And he who has seen has borne witness, and his witness is true; and he knows that he is telling the truth, so that you also may believe.
>
> (John 19:35 NASB)

It is natural for us to believe that this incident is to do with our salvation; but the fact of the matter is simple: Jesus had already won our salvation; and the veil in the temple had already been torn in two to signify that fact.

What then was so significant that John solemnly emphasizes it? It was the fact that the Second man, the New man, had been put to sleep; and, by the blood and water that came out of His side, a bride and a wife had been produced. It was as if the Lord Jesus was saying, "This is *ishah*, woman, for she was taken out of *ish*, man. This is bone of My bone and flesh of My flesh. This is Me!" That this is the truth to which John bore witness, is confirmed by what he writes in his first letter, when he states,

> This is he that came by water and blood, even Jesus Christ; not with the water only, but with the water and with the blood. And it is the Spirit that beareth witness, because the Spirit is the truth. For there are three who bear witness, the Spirit, and the water, and the blood: and the three agree in one.
>
> (1 John 5:6–8)

John saw something that happened on the cross *after Jesus had won our salvation*. What he saw, he understood as going to the very heart of God's purpose. Through the resurrection life of Christ, and His atoning blood, the Holy Spirit produces the Church as the body of the Lord Jesus. At Pentecost, the Holy Spirit was poured out and turned one hundred and twenty units of a near perfect but static congregation into one hundred and twenty members of the living body of the Lord Jesus. Livingly joined to the Head, they were to turn Jerusalem upside down, and then Judea and Samaria, and, finally, the Roman Empire!

Three materials out of which the city is built

In the first three chapters of the Bible, we have the mysterious but significant mention of three materials: gold, bdellium, and

onyx. The only way you can discover these materials is by
following the course of the river. They are not immediately
apparent, but have to be found, to be mined, or to be discovered. In the last three chapters, there are only three materials
out of which the New Jerusalem, the city of God, the bride,
the wife of the Lamb, is produced. They are gold, precious
stone, and pearl: gold, out of which the whole is created, transparent as crystal; precious stone, which constitutes the wall
of the city and its twelve foundations; and twelve huge single
pearls, out of which each of the twelve gates is built.

Gold

In the Word of God, gold signifies divine life and nature. Gold
in its raw state is found normally in river beds. Generally, it is
not apparent to the naked eye: it has to be sifted out of the soil
or sand. Only then can the process begin of refining it. The Lord
Jesus, speaking to the church in Laodicea about spiritual character, said: "I counsel thee to buy of me gold refined by fire,
that thou mayest become rich" (Revelation 3:18). A person with
spiritual character is spiritually and eternally rich! The gold, out
of which the city of God is produced, is refined beyond any gold
that we have ever seen: it is transparent as crystal or glass! This
represents something totally of God, given by His grace alone,
through the finished work of the Lord Jesus. Nevertheless, it is
worked in us through deep and often costly experience. The
fact that it is refined to a degree which makes it as transparent as crystal, denotes this. We should also note the amount of
gold that was used in both the tabernacle and the temple. This
gold was a type, or a picture, of the indwelling of Christ in the
Church and in the believer.

Once we begin to see this, a whole number of Scriptures take
on a deeper meaning for us. For example:

we have this treasure in earthen vessels . . .

(2 Corinthians 4:7)

for in him dwelleth all the fulness of the Godhead bodily, and in him ye are made full . . .

(Colossians 2:9–10)

For to me to live is Christ, and to die is gain.

(Philippians 1:21)

to whom God was pleased to make known what is the riches of the glory of this mystery among the Gentiles, which is Christ in you, the hope of glory . . .

(Colossians 1:27)

Pearl

What is bdellium? The Hebrew is *bedolach*. It is normally translated as bdellium. This is an aromatic plant which, when broken, exudes a resinous gum that hardens into a yellowish-white color and looks something like a pearl. We are told in the book of Exodus that manna was like frost on the ground, like coriander seed, white in color (see Exodus 16:14, 31). The book of Numbers records:

Now the manna was like coriander seed, and its appearance like that of bdellium.

(11:7 NASB)

There has been much discussion, both amongst the rabbis and amongst Christian Bible scholars, as to whether this *bedolach* is a plant or a river pearl. Let me quote one of the great authorities of the past, Gesenius. He states,

Now the modern authorities call it resinous gum from a tree, but I am not at all sure. On the other hand, bdellium is not such a precious natural production as to be mentioned between gold and precious stones and that the land of Havilah should be celebrated for producing it. On this account the opinion of the Jews is not to be rejected which has been learnedly supported by Bogart. The pearls are to be understood, of which a very large quantity are fished up in the Persian Gulf and in India, and with these it would not be unthinkable to compare the grains of manna. Bogart also gives the etymology as from the *bedal*, an excellent or selected pearl.

Whatever the truth is, we have a mysterious substance that looks very much like pearl, if it is not pearl. My own conviction is that we have here fresh water pearls. In the same manner in which gold and precious stone is not apparent to the naked eye, so we have pearls! One has to follow the course of the river to discover them: the pearls are within clams on the river bed. Furthermore, pearls are produced by a little worthless piece of grit falling into the softest part of the clam. The whole clam is then energized to rid itself of the intruder. It does so by coating the grit many times with a substance which finally forms a precious and costly pearl.

Of what does this speak? It surely signifies the kind of affliction which is given to certain believers and produces, in the end, something of incredible beauty and value. The apostle Paul's "thorn in the flesh" comes into this category.

These pearls, with their hidden history, are the gates of the city of God. The Word of God states that "each one of the gates was a single pearl" (Revelation 21:21b NASB). Those gates were not produced out of clusters of small pearls, or a few pearls together: they were each one an unbelievably large pearl. That gives us the clue to the hidden history in their creation. Some piece of worthless debris has been coated thousands of times to produce such pearls!

In many ways, gates were the most important part of a city, especially in the ancient world, where the elders sat in the gate for judgment. It was the place for the administration of government and law, and therefore extremely important to the whole life of the city.

Precious stones

If we follow the river, we are told, we shall find onyx stone. The Hebrew is *shoham*. We have a problem because the Hebrew is translated by the names of a number of different gem stones: for example, chrysophase, beryl, onyx, and, more recently, carnelian. Until recently, onyx has been the favored term. We can state with certainty that, whatever gem stone it was, it was precious or semi-precious stone.

In Exodus 28:9–12, it is recorded,

> And thou shalt take two onyx stones, and grave on them the names of the children of Israel: six of their names on the one stone, and the names of the six that remain on the other stone, according to their birth. With the work of an engraver in stone, like the engravings of a signet, shalt thou engrave the two stones, according to the names of the children of Israel: thou shalt make them to be inclosed in settings of gold. And thou shalt put the two stones upon the shoulder-pieces of the ephod, to be stones of memorial for the children of Israel: and Aaron shall bear their names before the Lord upon his two shoulders for a memorial.

Now we make a discovery. Whatever the gemstone was, whether onyx, chrysophase, beryl, or carnelian, in one sense, it does not really matter. On each one of the twelve gemstones of the breastplate, one of the names of the twelve tribes of Israel was engraved. The high priest bore the whole people of God on his heart before the Lord. All the meaning of these twelve precious stones was then summed up in the two onyx stones, which were borne one on each shoulder of the high priest. He bore the whole people of God on his shoulders as well as on his heart! Thus the onyx stones represent all precious stones. If we follow the river of life, we find not only gold and pearl, but precious stone.

Precious stone is normally produced by enormous heat and intense pressure in the dark places of the earth. This speaks of the beauties and glories of the Lord Jesus, which He works in those whom He saves. Isaiah promises:

> O thou afflicted, tossed with tempest, and not comforted, behold, I will set thy stones in fair colors, and lay thy foundations with sapphires. And I will make thy pinnacles of rubies . . . and all thy border of precious stones.
>
> (Isaiah 54:11–12)

Wood, hay, and stubble: a contrast

The only materials out of which the New Jerusalem, the wife of the Lamb, is created, are gold, precious stone, and pearl. There is no wood, or hay, or stubble.

Many years ago, I was taken by dear friends in the Philippines to see the V.I.P. guesthouse of the Philippines' government, built by Imelda Marcos and popularly called "The Coconut Palace." Everything within that beautiful building was made from the coconut palm tree: from the floor to the staircases, from the carpets to the lampshades, from chairs to tables, etc. It was all created from the coconut palm. It was very tasteful, elegant, and beautiful. It was, however, all "wood, hay, and stubble," like many a church and many a Christian life. There are many "coconut palaces" produced by the flesh, and not the Spirit.

There is no wood, hay, or stubble in the city of God. It is produced, as I have already written, out of only three materials: gold, precious stone, and pearl. They are in an altogether different dimension from that of wood, hay, and stubble! The three former materials all speak of the character, the nature, and the life of the Lord Jesus. They speak of what the Holy Spirit, the

Builder of the city of God, the New Jerusalem, has to produce in us. The latter three materials speak of the work of the flesh: sometimes brilliant, creative, energetic, and striking, but corruptible. There is, however, one serious problem; there is a *divine veto* on wood, hay, and stubble!

The Spirit and the Bride say, "Come"

In the first three chapters of the Bible, there is pain, sorrow, and death; in the last three chapters, there are those wonderful words:

> and he shall wipe away every tear from their eyes; and death shall be no more; neither shall there be mourning, nor crying, nor pain, any more: the first things are passed away.
>
> (Revelation 21:4)

In the first three chapters, time is ushered in; and in the last three chapters, eternity is ushered in.

Then there is one last and marvelous correspondence between the beginning and the end of the Bible. In the first three chapters, we have an extraordinary picture of the Spirit of God. It is recorded: "the Spirit of God moved upon the face of the waters" (Genesis 1:2). The Hebrew translated in English as "moved" is *rachaf*. It speaks of a bird of prey hovering, looking for a roosting place, a nest! It even has the idea of "brooding." When we speak of a "broody" hen, we mean a hen that wants to have chicks.

In another place, the same Hebrew word is used:

> As an eagle that stirreth up her nest, that fluttereth over her young, He spread abroad his wings, he took them,
> He bare them on his pinions.
>
> (Deuteronomy 32:11)

"Fluttereth over her young" is the word *rachaf*, translated in Genesis 1:2 as "hovereth" or "broodeth." As I have said, this is an extraordinary picture. It has the idea of affection, of love, of bringing new life, and cherishing that new life; of finding and building a dwelling place, a home!

At the beginning of the divine record of creation, it is stated: "the earth was waste and void; and darkness was upon the face of the deep . . . " (Genesis 1:2). Then we have this picture of the Holy Spirit looking for a resting place, a home. The Holy Spirit, whilst always at work throughout the whole of the Old Testament time, never found that home on earth. In one sense, at least in figure, He found it when, at the dedication of the tabernacle, and later of the temple, the glory of the Lord filled both of them. It was only when the Lord Jesus was born that the Holy Spirit found his home on this earth and that fact was confirmed at His baptism, and the beginning of His Messianic ministry. John the Baptist declared: "I have beheld the Spirit descending as a dove out of heaven; and it abode upon him" (John 1:32).

When the Holy Spirit was poured out by the glorified and risen Messiah at Pentecost, the Holy Spirit came home to a redeemed people, saved and joined to the Messiah. He came not merely to visit them, or to use them, or even merely to empower them, but to dwell in them permanently!

When we come to the last three chapters of the Bible, in the very last chapter, almost the last verses, there are these wonderful words: "And the Spirit and the Bride say, Come" (Revelation 22:17a). It is almost as if the Holy Spirit has finally produced what, from the very beginning, God had intended in His heart. It is so simply and beautifully put: "the Spirit and the bride say, Come." Behind those words are thousands of years of the seeking and the working of the Holy Spirit. Now, there is no more "hovering" and no more "brooding": the work is done, and the bride is there beside Him to prove that His work is finally accomplished.

Chapter 4

HE HATH SET ETERNITY IN THEIR HEART

As we have seen in the previous chapter, the extraordinary correspondence between the beginning and the end of the Bible reveals a very definite design. It is in the comprehension of that design that we are brought into an understanding of the Eternal Purpose of God.

The Bible begins with a human marriage and ends with a divine one; it begins with a marriage that is "till death parts," and ends with one that is forever; it begins with a marriage between two human beings, and ends with a marriage between the Lamb, the Messiah, and the bride, the wife of the Lamb. This truth brings us to the heart of the matter. The fact that the Bible is a divine love story begins to dawn upon us at this point.

It is not only the correspondence between the beginning and the end of the Bible that is so remarkable: in the Jewish Greek arrangement (LXX) and the Christian arrangement of the Bible, at its heart we find two little books: Ecclesiastes and the Song of Songs. Over both of them there has been much discussion. The Song of Songs has been described by some liberal theologians as a bawdy Middle East ditty. The traditional Jewish view of it was totally different. It was held that it was a vision, or allegory, which God gave to King Solomon in a dream, describing the love between God and His own. Over many years, Ecclesiastes was the focal point of heated discussion by the rabbis as to whether it should even be included in the Canon of Scripture. Many of them pointed out that it hardly mentions God, or the Torah, or even salvation. Its theme song, "vanity, vanity, all is vanity," seems oddly out of line with the rest of Scripture. Some have pointed out that it is an ancient form of a modern philosophy: Jean Paul Sartre's existentialism: "What is the point of anything? All is empty and futile; eat, drink, and be merry, for tomorrow we die!"

It seems clear that these two little books belong to one another. One is negative, and the other is positive. One describes fallen mankind, his futile life and his end; and the other describes those whom God redeems and brings into an eternal covenant relationship with Himself.

"He hath set eternity in their heart . . . "

Ecclesiastes is perfectly described by its theme: "vanity, vanity, all is vanity." The Hebrew word translated "vanity" literally means "vapor." This word vanity appears thirty-eight times throughout this little book. It is translated in English as "vanity, vanity, all is vanity" but could also be translated "perfect, or utter vanity, all is vanity." It describes the utter emptiness and futility of an unsaved life, alienated and divorced from God: it is "perfect emptiness, all is emptiness!", "perfect futility, all is futility!"

Here at the heart of the Bible we have this testimony of the useless and empty futility of a life lived without God. That kind of life amounts to nothing. You can erect marvelous buildings; you can lay out magnificent parks and gardens; you can make money and prosper; you can pursue a career and come to its zenith; you can buy much property; you can achieve many academic degrees and titles; you can lose yourself in sexual pleasure; you can even be over righteous; in the end, however, it amounts to nothing. The insubstantial nature of sinful and fallen man renders it all vanity, or vapor. There is another phrase in this little book which also explains its message, and is associated with the word "vanity": it is "striving after wind." This occurs nine times within it, and vividly defines the total futility and emptiness of a life lived without God.

Then in the midst of all that is so depressingly negative, we have a statement that, in my estimation, is the key to the whole book:

> He hath made everything beautiful in its time: also he hath set eternity in their heart, yet so that man cannot find out the work that God hath done from the beginning even to the end.
>
> (Ecclesiastes 3:11)

The Hebrew word *olam*, here translated "eternity," means "eternal," "age lasting," or "forever." God has placed this "foreverness" in the heart of man. At the very beginning, when God created man, He breathed into him spirit and created an eternal dimension to his being. That eternity in the heart of fallen man is a "God-shaped" vacuum or blank. It can only be filled by the Lord. If it is filled with other things: money, sport, sex, career, or anything else other than the Lord, then that fallen human being can never be satisfied. That kind of life becomes meaningless. Only when the Lord fills the vacuum can a person begin to understand from the beginning to the end what God has purposed.

> I know that, whatsoever God doeth, it shall be for ever; nothing can be put to it, nor anything taken from it: and God hath done it . . .
>
> (Ecclesiastes 3:14)

When the Lord steps into that vacuum within an unsaved man or woman, He does a work that is eternal! One can neither add to it, nor subtract from it.

My beloved is mine and I am His

When we turn to the little book entitled the Song of Songs, we find an altogether different picture. Here all is full of purpose and meaning. There is no endless cycle of futility and vanity, but instead a marvelous progress to the throne. It is the story of a shepherdess taken from a humble home and simple beginnings, and married to the king himself. Then, step by step, one begins to see the most amazing process of education and instruction, leading to reigning with the king. It is an incredible process of training and discipline, which in turn results in maturity and responsibility. Far from anything futile, empty, or vain, that process is full of value, purpose, and meaning.

Within this little song, we have three refrains, which mark the progress of the bride. The first refrain is: "My beloved is mine, and I am his . . . " (Song of Songs 2:16). That sums up so much of modern ego-centric Christianity: Christ is *mine*! It is all mine: *my* crown, *my* joy, *my* peace, *my* satisfaction, *my* fulfillment, *my* work, *my* pulpit, *my* church, *my* ministry, *my* gifts! The fact is, none of us would have ever been saved if the Lord had not played on this self-centeredness which characterizes all of us. The Lord loves us so much that He went along with that self-centeredness in order to save us. We were saved because we were in need, and He alone had the answer to that need. I have traveled all over the world, and I have yet to find a single person who has been saved simply because they loved God with all their heart and wanted to please and serve Him! Every one whom I have met, who has been born of God, was saved out of a sense of hopelessness and inability, out of great need.

At this stage in our experience, everything in the church, and in our Christian life and service revolves around us and centers in us. We, of course, do believe that *we are His*, but it is a muted and secondary testimony. The main emphasis is "my beloved is *mine*."

I am my beloved's, and my beloved is mine

Then the Lord begins to deal with our self-centered Christianity, and we come to the second refrain in this little book: "I am my beloved's, and my beloved is mine . . . " (Song of Songs 6:3). The order of priorities is changing! Her beloved comes and knocks on the door, but she says, "Well, he is mine. I will take my time. I have a permanent and stable relationship, and I am not going to lose it. He can wait." When finally she rises, smelling her own perfume, she opens the door and he is gone! That is a shock. She no longer senses his nearness and feels that maybe he has deserted her. Then she goes out into the streets looking for him. She gets beaten up by different groups and left for half dead, until finally he comes to her again. He is bringing her to a new position in her relationship with himself. It is at this point that her refrain changes: "I am my beloved's, and my beloved is mine." The emphasis is now on her beloved, and not so much on her.

All of this is an amazing picture of the way the Lord deals with those whom He loves and saves! At this point in our Christian life, the Lord begins to challenge us to lay down our lives; to become living sacrifices; to give up all right to our self-life; to take up our cross and to follow Him. Then it is no longer *my* joy, *my* peace, *my* satisfaction, *my* will, and what *I want*. Now it is *His* joy, *His* peace, *His* satisfaction, *His* purpose, *His* fulfillment, *His* work, *His* will, and what *He wants*! Spiritually we are growing up and are beginning to take responsibility for the things of God, and for the people of God, and for the unsaved world around us.

I am my beloved's and His desire is towards me

Then we come to the last refrain: "I am my beloved's; and his desire is toward me" (Song of Songs 7:10). The loved one no longer speaks of what is hers, but only that she belongs to him, and that his desire is toward her. She has lost the sense of insecurity that caused her to express continuously that she possessed him; and that, what was his, was hers. Finally she has come to a position of complete trust and rest concerning her relationship with her beloved. He now means and is everything to her! It is beautifully expressed in one sentence: "Who is this that cometh up from the wilderness, leaning upon her beloved?" (Song of Songs 8:5). She has found her all in him and is at rest in his love. We have here an amazing and tender picture of the way the Lord Himself brings those He has saved to the place where He is everything to them.

For the first time in this little book, we discover that she is concerned for someone else!

> We have a little sister, and she hath no breasts: What shall we do for our sister in the day when she shall be spoken for?
>
> (Song of Songs 8:8)

Never before has the bride shown any concern for anyone other than herself. Her beloved has, at last, weaned her away from her natural and spontaneous self-centeredness, and her bondage to self-interest and to her own well-being. This reveals spiritual maturity. She has grown up! Who is this little sister, if it is not those believers who have not spiritually grown up? Thus ends the Song of Songs.

"Simon, son of John, do you love Me?"

It is remarkable that the apostle John concludes his gospel in much the same way. The Gospel of John is not a history, although it is historically accurate. It is an interpretation. It is, therefore, of great significance that he brings his testimony almost to its completion with the story of the Lord Jesus meeting the restored but still broken Peter. Jesus asked him: "Simon, son of John, do you love Me more than these?" (John 21:15

NASB). The old Peter would have answered in a very different manner to the manner in which he now answers Him. Peter could not even use the same Greek word that the Lord Jesus used. The Lord had used the Greek *agapao,* which means to love unselfishly, to the extent of self-sacrifice. Peter could not rise to that level and, instead, uses another Greek word, *phileo,* with a good but a much lesser meaning. It means to be a friend and to have the same interests. Peter answers, "Yes, Lord; You know that I love You": You know that I have real affection for You and share Your concerns! The Lord then says: "Tend My lambs." Three times the Lord asked him the same question, twice using *agapao*; and the third and the last time He came down to Peter's level and used the same word as Peter, *phileo.*

Every time Peter answered the Messiah, Jesus commanded him to tend His lambs, or shepherd His sheep, or tend His sheep. The Lord was seeking to emphasize that our love for Him *has* to be expressed in our love and care for others. In this way our love for the Lord Jesus is alone evidenced. In principle, this is the same great lesson as that of the Song of Songs: "We have a little sister . . ."

The sign at the wedding in Cana

We have not only discovered that the Bible begins with a marriage and ends with a marriage, one earthly and the other heavenly, we have also discovered at the heart of the Bible there is another wedding, another marriage. This is found in these two little books dealing with the whole question of eternal purpose: one negatively and the other positively.

Now we make another discovery. The Gospel of John, as I have already written, is not one of the three synoptic or historical gospels (Matthew, Mark, and Luke), but stands on its own as a supreme interpretation of the life and work of the Lord Jesus. John builds this interpretation on the eight great claims of the Lord Jesus, all beginning with "I am," and eight great miracles which he selects and calls "signs." In other words, he understood those miracles as signifying great and foundational truths.

He records that the Messiah performed the *first* sign of His Messianic ministry at a wedding in Cana of Galilee (see John 2:1–11). The three years of the Messianic ministry of the Lord Jesus, which was to end in His supreme work at Calvary, began at a wedding and a marriage.

Unbelievably someone had not properly done their home-work: there was not enough wine at the wedding for the guests. Possibly many more came than had been anticipated. This would have been entirely possible in an ancient Jewish wed-ding since the whole area and beyond was normally invited! Whatever the reason, it was first and foremost a disaster for any Jewish wedding! Mary, the mother of Jesus, quietly told Him about the problem, but He seemed unconcerned. With a wom-an's intuition, she said to the servants: "Whatever He says to you, do it."

At some point not long afterwards, Jesus told those servants to fill the large stone pots with water, and then He turned what was corruptible water into incorruptible wine. It was not col-ored water, or "sacramental wine," or unfermented grape juice, or blackcurrant juice, all of which are corruptible. It was the very best vintage wine and was recognized as such by those present!

An essential and foundational truth is expressed by this first sign of the Messianic ministry of the Lord Jesus. Whatever may be our feeling about wine, one thing is clear and certain: the Lord Jesus turns the corruptible water of our fallen life into the incorruptible wine of His life. When He enters our being with eternal life, He brings the incorruptible into us! With Him, we inherit incorruption.

Why did the apostle John select this as the first sign unless he believed that the heart of God's purpose is related to a wedding? Interestingly, John the Baptist described himself as the "friend of the bridegroom." In Western terms, he was calling himself the "Best Man." He said,

> He that hath the bride is the bridegroom: but the friend of the bridegroom, that standeth and heareth him, rejoiceth greatly because of the bridegroom's voice: this my joy therefore is made full.
>
> (John 3:29)

An eternal and glorious marriage

The Bible ends with a wedding, and that is the reason why John selected a wedding as the first sign. What the Lamb and the wife of the Lamb will do in the eternal ages to come is not revealed to us. It is enough for us to know that God will reach that wedding and the marriage. The Bible, with its incredible revelation of God's heart and mind, ends with these two, the Lamb and His bride, going forward into eternity. How greatly Satan and his hierarchy have sought to frustrate that purpose of God, and failed! What colossal battles and intense conflict lie behind this marriage! The glorious objective has finally been reached, and the Lamb and the wife of the Lamb now move forward to their thrilling destiny.

The Bible uses a word for this: it is the word "glory." Many times Bible teachers and preachers have tried to use another word for glory, to make its meaning more clear. In my estimation, nothing else works! The Spirit of God has to reveal the meaning of *glory* to the child of God. The apostle Peter has summed it all up in the words: "the God of all grace, who called you unto his eternal glory in Christ . . . " (1 Peter 5:10). This glory is found alone in Christ: He is the focal point of God's glory, the center and the circumference of it. Essentially, glory is God *at home*. It is the tangible and substantial manifestation of the presence of God. Glory is always manifested when God is fully satisfied!

It is clear from the Word of God that the Lord Jesus is the key to both the creation of the universe and the creation of man.

> [Christ] who is the image of the invisible God, the firstborn of all creation; for in him were all things created, in the heavens, and upon the earth, things visible and things invisible, whether thrones or dominions or principalities or powers; all things have been created through him, and unto him; and he is before all things, and in him all things hold together [mg].
>
> (Colossians 1:15–17)

When the wedding is finally celebrated, then the glory of God will fill the whole earth: the natural creation will be released into the freedom of the glory of the children of God; and the knowledge of the glory of God will cover the earth as the waters cover the sea. It is all glory!

We have to remember that the Spirit of God uses "Sunday school" language when He speaks of this wedding and marriage. A "wedding" is a universally understood picture, whatever one's color, or race, or culture, or background. Everyone understands the words "marriage" and "wedding." The Lord uses this simple picture to convey profound and fathomless truth: eternal and spiritual union and communion with God in Christ is the reality.

There are thousands of questions that children of God have about eternity to come: Will we recognize one another? What kind of bodies will we have? Will we wear clothes? Will we eat food? What will be the work we will do? There are some indications in the Scriptures that might enable us to answer some of these questions, but most if not all of our answers would be basically speculative. It is, in fact, just as well that we have not been given full answers or we would have that many more denominations! Suffice it to state that God has not grown weary or tired. His creative genius is as fresh, as alive, and as energetic as it was at the beginning of time. If He could have created something as amazing as this planet, still a marvel even in its disfigured and polluted state, what will it be when He gets down to the real work of eternity?

The Bible concludes with an eternal marriage. It is almost as if the Lord is saying, "You can leave all the many questions you have with Me. It is enough for you to know that you belong to Me and will reign with Me throughout the ages to come. Take My hand and walk with Me, and trust Me with all your questions. I promise you that it will be far more wonderful and glorious than you have ever thought or dreamed!"

Chapter 5

THE HOLY CITY,
THE NEW JERUSALEM

The whole revelation of God's heart and mind in the Bible ends with the celebration of a wedding and a marriage. As has already been pointed out, this is a remarkable and significant conclusion to the sixty-six books which constitute our Bible. It is both striking and meaningful because it combines two very different ideas in one.

John testified:

> And I saw a new heaven and a new earth: for the first heaven and the first earth are passed away; and the sea is no more. And I saw the holy city, new Jerusalem, coming down out of heaven of God, made ready as a bride adorned for her husband.
>
> (Revelation 21:1–2)

Take careful note of the words "the holy city, new Jerusalem . . . made ready as a bride adorned for her husband." He continues with his testimony:

> and he spake with me, saying, Come hither, I will show thee the bride, the wife of the Lamb. And he carried me away in the Spirit to a mountain great and high, and showed me the holy

city Jerusalem, coming down out of heaven from God, having the glory of God . . .

(Revelation 21:9–11)

Again note the words "the bride, the wife of the Lamb . . . the holy city Jerusalem . . ."

We have here two diametrically different ideas: on the one hand, a capital city and, on the other hand, a bride and a wife. We do not normally associate these two ideas with each other. A capital city is not a bride! A bride is not a capital city! I have traveled all over the world and have been introduced at different times to thousands of wives by their husbands. No loving husband has ever yet introduced his wife as his "capital city," although, on occasion, some of those wives have been built like fortresses, and the government and treasury are obviously located in them! These two concepts, of a wife and a capital city, do not naturally belong to one another.

What is it that the Lord is seeking to say through this? As I see it, it is in the understanding of the combination of these two truths that we begin to recognize the practical outworking of God's Eternal Purpose in our lives. In this chapter, we shall consider "the holy city, the New Jerusalem."

A capital city is the center, the headquarters, of national government and administration. A nation is governed from its capital; it is there that national policies and laws are defined and administered. Whether a kingdom or a republic, it is the heart of that state, and can also be the hub of an empire. The New Jerusalem is alone the capital of the kingdom of God and His Messiah; from there all will be governed and administered.

There can be little doubt that the government of God will be centered in a physical and literal headquarters in a new heaven and a new earth. However, the description we have of this capital city in Revelation 21 and 22 seems to be symbolic rather than literal. For example, there is only one street, but there are twelve gates. It can be argued that the one street is a spiraling circular street; but how do you reach the many homes, markets, and offices in the city? There are no other lanes or streets mentioned! We are even told that, in the midst of that one street, "a river of water of life" proceeds, with the tree of life on either side of it.

The extraordinary thing about this city is that its measurements are four square: it is a cube. It is as long as it is broad as it is high. We are given the exact measurement: 12,000 furlongs, i.e. 1,400 miles, or 2,200 kilometers. It is 1,400 miles long and 1,400 miles wide and 1,400 miles high; and yet it has only one street and twelve gates. The New Jerusalem is therefore approximately twice the size of the state of Texas in the United States, and about the same size as the Republic of South Africa.

The holy of holies in the tabernacle and in the temple were both four square: they were shaped as a cube. The meaning is obvious: this capital city is the dwelling place of God and of His glory. It is the Holy of Holies! In this capital city, there is no temple, no chapel, no "church" building, and no synagogue. We are told simply that the Lord God and the Lamb are the temple thereof (see Revelation 21:22). This is the place from which He will reveal Himself and express Himself to the whole universe and beyond.

There is another interesting fact: everything in this capital city is related to the number twelve, or a multiple thereof. There are twelve gates, twelve angels, twelve tribes, twelve foundations, twelve apostles of the Lamb, 12,000 furlongs, 144 cubits (twelve times twelve), twelve pearls, and twelve manner of fruits, and twelve times a year that the tree of life produces those fruits. In biblical numerology, twelve is the figure or number of government, of reigning and ruling, and of divine authority.

Thus we have a further confirmation that this New Jerusalem, this city of God, is related to spiritual government and authority. This city represents that great company of the redeemed whom the Lord will have brought, through much discipline and trial, to the place where they can reign with Him from His throne.

Christ, the Divine Amen to the fulfillment of God's purpose

It is entirely noteworthy that the glorified, risen Messiah, the Lord Jesus, concludes the seven messages He gave to the seven churches with the words:

> He that overcometh, I will give to him to sit down with me in my throne, as I also overcame, and sat down with my Father in his throne. He that hath an ear, let him hear what the Spirit saith to the churches.
>
> (Revelation 3:21–22)

He gathers up everything that He has said in these concluding words. It is clear from them that the Lord's purpose is not only to save us, but to bring us to reign with Him in His throne. When He said: "as I also overcame, and sat down with my Father in his throne," we know with certainty that He reigns with the Father. The goal of His salvation is to bring us to reign with Himself.

It is wonderfully strengthening and encouraging to those who want to be faithful in the last days that the Lord spoke these words to a church that was anything but faithful. It was to the church at Laodicea. Abject failure, affluent lukewarmness, spiritual blindness, and an arrogant self-sufficiency characterized that fellowship! Unbelievably, the Head of the church, and the Savior of the body, was outside of it, knocking on the door, and saying:

> if any man hear my voice and open the door, I will come in to him, and will sup with him, and he with me.
>
> (Revelation 3:20)

It is mind-blowing that a church worshiping the Lord Jesus, studying His Word and remembering Him in the breaking of bread, had not the faintest idea that the Head of the church was outside of their organization! They thought they were rich and had need of nothing whilst, in fact, He described them as "the wretched one and miserable and poor and blind and naked." I have already mentioned in a previous chapter the discrepancy between their self-estimate and the Lord's appraisal of their true condition. Sadly, this is an appalling and accurate description of so much of the Church in our day!

In spite of all this failure, the Lord still calls any who are faithful in Laodicea to open the door, that He may come in and share precious fellowship with them. Even more amazing is the fact that this kind of intimate fellowship could lead us, by His grace and power, to be enthroned with Him. Thus, even though surrounded by failure, one can reach the fulfillment of His Eternal Purpose. In fact, the very surrounding failure in both the unsaved world and even in the church can be the catalyst that will drive the faithful to reach God's goal.

It comes as an enormous encouragement, therefore, to recognize the titles with which the Messiah, the Head of the Church, introduces Himself to the church at Laodicea. He speaks of Himself as the Amen, the Faithful and True Witness, and the Beginning of the Creation of God. The Lord Jesus is the Amen of God. In Him, the Father has secured and realized His Eternal Purpose; and by the Holy Spirit that purpose will be practically fulfilled through Him. Christ is the guarantee, the Divine Amen to its fulfillment.

Christ the Faithful and True Witness

He speaks of Himself as "the Faithful and True Witness." The book of Revelation has a phrase which is hardly found anywhere else in the Bible, "the testimony of Jesus." The church at Laodicea had contradicted that, and, in fact, the lampstand which signifies that testimony, was probably in danger of being removed. It is hard to believe that it would still remain in its place when the Lord Jesus was outside of the church, and His voice was being ignored by it. Yet the Lord Jesus remained the Faithful and True Witness at Laodicea, even if *they* were neither faithful nor true. To all who long to see God's Eternal Purpose fulfilled, this is of tremendous encouragement.

The beginning of the creation of God

The Lord Jesus is also the beginning of the creation of God. The apostle Paul declared:

> Wherefore if any man is in Christ, there is a new creation [mg]: the old things are passed away; behold, they are become new. But all things are of God . . .
>
> (2 Corinthians 5:17–18)

The problem with the church at Laodicea was that it had sources other than the Lord Jesus, sources that were in this world: in its fashion, in its philosophy, in its psychology, and in its way of doing things. Those alien sources always lead to mixture, compromise, and spiritual defilement. They inevitably lead to a wretched condition, to blindness, to nakedness, and to spiritual poverty. However negative and depressing the condition may be in the church at Laodicea, the Lord still calls those who are faithful, to follow Him to the end and come finally to reign with Him in His throne. All His immense and fathomless grace, and all the exceeding greatness of the power of the Holy Spirit, is made available to them, whatever the conditions around them may be.

It is your Father's good pleasure to give you the kingdom

It is clear that, in saving us, the Lord has called us to reign with Christ. The Lord Jesus declared:

> Fear not, little flock; for it is your Father's good pleasure to give you the kingdom.
>
> (Luke 12:32)

These words do not merely convey the idea of being *in* the kingdom: there is also within them the suggestion of reigning with Christ. It is not *only* the kingdom, but also kingship! When the Lord Jesus spoke of sitting down with Him in His throne, He simply meant that we are to rule with Him.

This matter of reigning with the Lord is everywhere in the Bible. In its simplest form, we discover it in the first chapters: the Lord said:

> Be fruitful, and multiply, and replenish the earth, and subdue it; and have dominion over the fish of the sea and over the birds of the heavens, and over every living thing that moveth upon the earth.
>
> (Genesis 1:28)

The word "to have dominion" simply means to rule. Man was not only to multiply; he was to subdue the earth, to replenish it, and to rule over it.

It is interesting to consider the condition of the earth at its beginning and before the Fall. Was it perfect, with everything in its right place, or was it a riot of life, rambling and growing everywhere? We are told that the Lord Himself created a garden and planted it, and took Adam and put him into the garden to dress it and keep it, or guard it (see Genesis 2:8, 15). Adam and Eve were not to be at the mercy of the elements, nor to feel threatened by the riotous abundance of the natural creation. They were to rule over it; they were to subdue it and to replenish it. It seems to me that this beautiful garden was an allotment, which the Lord Himself created within that "unfallen" paradise of life. If Adam and Eve had not fallen, but had instead trusted the Lord, in union with the Lord they probably would have added allotment to allotment, until they gradually ruled the whole earth. It would have been the first stages of training for reigning with Christ in the ages to come. This is, of course, speculative!

What we know with certainty is that the Lord told them to have dominion and to rule. This is confirmed by the words of the psalmist concerning man and his place on the earth:

> . . . thou hast made him but little lower than God,
> And crownest him with glory and honor.
> Thou makest him to have dominion over the works of thy hands; Thou hast put all things under his feet . . .
>
> (Psalm 8:5–6)

From its simple beginning, we trace this matter throughout the Word of God, whether it is in having dominion, or in ruling, or in reigning, or in overcoming. It is summed up in the words of the Lord through Moses:

> And it shall come to pass, if thou shalt hearken diligently unto the voice of the Lord thy God, to observe all his command-ments which I command thee this day, that the Lord thy God shall set thee on high above all the nations of the earth . . . thou shalt lend unto many nations, and thou shalt not borrow. And the Lord will make thee the head, and not the tail; and thou shalt be above only, and thou shalt not be beneath . . .
>
> (Deuteronomy 28:1, 12–13)

Throughout the Word of God, we have the record of those whom the Lord called and enabled to overcome and reign with Him. Whether it is Abraham, or Jacob, or Joseph, or Moses, or Samuel, or David: the list is endless, even without the great number that could be added to it from the New Testament. From all of these, we learn that we do not easily come to this position of reigning with Him. Overcoming involves conflict. For this reason, the apostle Paul said to Timothy: "Fight the good fight of faith; take hold of the eternal life to which you were called . . ." (1 Timothy 6:12 NASB). We do not come hap-hazardly to the throne to reign with Christ. There is an enemy, and much conflict; and we have to *fight* the good fight and *take hold* of eternal life. The apostle, giving his testimony in another letter, writes: "that I may lay hold on that for which also I was laid hold on by Christ Jesus" (Philippians 3:12). He uses a very strong word, translated here "laid hold." Christ has laid hold of you for what? It is not only your so great salvation, but the goal of that salvation. You and I have to *lay hold on that* for which Christ also laid hold on us! We should note carefully the apostle's words: "if we endure, we shall also reign with him . . . " (2 Timothy 2:12). There is an "*if*" in this promise!

It is a fallacy, commonly held amongst many Christian believers, that we shall automatically come to the throne to reign with Christ. Neither a baby nor a child can reign. Even an adolescent would normally be disqualified. It is obvious from the many warnings and injunctions in the Word of God that we need to grow in the Lord and, if we are to reign, come to some minimal form of maturity. The idea that the Lord can wave a magic wand over us at death and transform a mean-hearted, crabby, narrow-minded, and self-centered Christian into a saint is a fairy tale! Someone who could not rule their relationships, or their own personal affairs, or their home, or their business life or workaday life, or even their pets is not likely suddenly to be given the position of ruling over regions of the earth. It is obvious that the child of God has to "grow in the grace and knowledge of our Lord and Saviour Jesus Christ" (2 Peter 3:18). You and I have to grow up spiritually.

Spiritual growth

The first essential, therefore, if we are to reign with Christ, is spiritual growth. We cannot remain spiritual babes, or spiritual kindergarten children, or even spiritual adolescents. He seeks those who will become His good soldiers. The Lord is looking for candidates for His throne who will grow up and become spiritual adults. To reign with Christ requires a certain maturity.

A babe, a child, or an adolescent cannot become prime minister, or president, or even, in practical performance, a king or a queen.

This is the problem which God faces. His kingdom is filled with babies, who never grow beyond childhood. There is nothing more beautiful than a baby, and babyhood and childhood are a natural and essential part of growing up. It is a period of time when everything and everyone circles around the baby and the baby's needs. It is the time for toys, for rattles, and for dummies or pacifiers; for anything, and everything, that pleases and satisfies our small minds and limited interests. At that stage in growth, there is always someone to rock the baby when he or she cries. However, if that baby is to grow up into a normal human being, there comes the need of discipline, of training, and of education. It is on these matters that the Word of God has so much to say. It is everywhere in the Bible, and if we ignore its commands and its warnings on this matter, we do so at our own risk.

When a person remains a baby or a child, even at twenty or forty years of age or more, it is no longer beautiful. It is abnormal and unnatural. Modern Christianity rarely goes beyond this stage of babyhood and childhood in experience: indeed, basically, it only caters for this stage. The result is a self-centered Christianity concerned mostly with its own needs and problems, and little concerned with service and sacrifice. Actually, the writer of the Hebrew letter addressed the same problem when he wrote:

> Concerning [Christ] we have much to say, and it is hard to explain, since you have become dull of hearing. For though by this time you ought to be teachers, you have need again for someone to teach you the elementary principles of the oracles of God, and you have come to need milk and not solid food. For everyone who partakes only of milk is not accustomed to the word of righteousness, for he is a babe. But solid food is for the mature, who because of practice have their senses trained to discern good and evil.
>
> (5:11–14 NASB)

It was this pathetic condition of permanent spiritual babyhood
which finally brought spiritual death to all that the Lord had
done in the first centuries of church history. The lesson we learn
is simple: there is no alternative to spiritual growth, and no substitute for spiritual maturity.

It was exactly this problem that burdened the apostle Paul
when he wrote: "My little children, of whom I am again in travail until Christ be formed in you . . . " (Galatians 4:19). He was
deeply concerned about the need of growth to maturity. He
expressed again that concern in another letter when he wrote
that believers should "attain . . . unto a fullgrown man, unto the
measure of the stature of the fulness of Christ: that we may be
no longer children . . . " (Ephesians 4:13–14).

Discipline and training

Another basic essential, if we are to reign with Christ, is
discipline and training. No one can come to the throne without
such discipline and training. The writer of the Hebrew letter
states:

> "My son, do not regard lightly the discipline of the Lord, nor
> faint when you are reproved by him; for those whom the Lord
> loves He disciplines, and He scourges every son whom He
> receives." It is for discipline that you endure; God deals with
> you as with sons; for what son is there whom his father does
> not discipline? . . . All discipline for the moment seems not to
> be joyful, but sorrowful; yet to those who have been trained by
> it, afterwards it yields the peaceful fruit of righteousness.
>
> (12:5–7, 11 NASB)

How does the Lord discipline us and train us? It is through the
situations and circumstances of normal life; through relationships in family life, in work life, in church life, and in the work
of God.

The apostle Paul, seeking to encourage and strengthen the disciples in many places, said: "through many tribulations we must enter into the kingdom of God" (Acts 14:22). He uses a word in Greek that comes from the idea of being crushed, or pressed, or squeezed, and means "grievous affliction or distress." These tribulations work in us a greater capacity for glory. They also produce an ability to govern wisely and sensitively. If we have been born again, we have surely already entered into the kingdom of God. What then does the apostle mean when he says that it is through these many tribulations that *we enter* the kingdom, unless he means that we are being prepared for kingship. The greater the responsibility we shall have in the eternal ages to come, the higher the position we shall occupy, the greater the tribulations we will have to endure. It is all to do with discipline and training. Consider what Paul himself had to endure. God put him into chains, when we would have had him in all the pulpits and on all the platforms of the world. Our brother Watchman Nee, with one of the greatest ministries in the history of the Church, suffered twenty-two years in prison and, in the end, died alone on a country road, with only the company of brutal and godless guards. There is no alternative to discipline and training, if we are to reign with Christ in the ages to come.

Spiritual education

Another basic essential in this matter is spiritual education. It is the Holy Spirit's work to educate those who will come to the throne. Potentially it is the calling of every believer to reign with Christ in the ages to come, but to reach that throne one has to follow Him fully, whatever the cost. It is an essential schooling for true disciples. All the treasures of wisdom and knowledge are hidden in the Lord Jesus, and it is the ministry of the Holy Spirit to educate us and to make those treasures a reality in our experience. Out of that education, a developed spiritual intelligence is produced, whereby we can discern the mind of the Lord and sense what is His will. It is for this reason that those who will come to the throne will always be involved in costly prayer and intercession. In genuine intercession, spiritual intelligence and discernment are vital, as also is wisdom. The lessons we learn in intercession are lessons learned forever!

Wisdom and a hearing ear

It is interesting to note that when the Lord appeared to Solomon, He said to him, "Ask what I shall give thee," and Solomon said, "Give me now wisdom and knowledge, that I may go out and come in before this people; for who can judge this thy people, that is so great?" (see 2 Chronicles 1:7–12). Note the order which Solomon gave: he placed "wisdom" first. In the parallel account recorded in 1 Kings 3:4–10, Solomon asked for an "understanding heart." The Hebrew is literally "a hearing ear." This takes us to the heart of the matter. I have already written about the difference between knowledge and wisdom in the first chapter. If we are to reign with Christ, we need both knowledge and wisdom: knowledge is to do with facts, and wisdom is to do with the handling of those facts. Wisdom always comes from a spiritual hearing ear.

When I was saved at a young age and first began to read the Bible, I could not understand why Aaron and Moses were always falling on their faces before the Lord when confronted with problems. It seemed to me that they were the only two people who had the knowledge and wisdom to know what to do with the serious problems that confronted them. Now much later in life, I understand and it is no longer a mystery to me. It was not the facts that bothered them; it was how to handle the facts. They needed to *hear the counsel* of the Lord. From that hearing ear comes wisdom. In this connection, it is interesting to note that the Lord ends every one of the seven messages to the churches with the words: "he that hath an ear, let him hear what the Spirit saith to the churches."

When the Lord met me and saved me, just before I was thirteen years of age, I wanted to know everything! I was full of questions and a determination to find the answers. I tired out everyone in the church with my queries. A dear and beloved old Swedish sister saw my youthful arrogance and said to me that what I needed was not merely knowledge but wisdom. For exactly your condition, she said, there is a promise in God's Word:

> But if any of you lacketh wisdom, let him ask of God, who giveth to all liberally and upbraideth not; and it shall be given him. But let him ask in faith, nothing doubting . . .
>
> (James 1:5–6)

It sank deeply into my heart, and I stood on that promise every day for at least ten years, claiming it before the Lord. For anyone in a condition like mine, this promise is yes in Christ, and through Him is the Amen (see 2 Corinthians 1:20).

The Lord uses all the normal circumstances of our life to bring us to the place where we are the head and not the tail, we are above and not beneath. There is no alternative or substitute for the lifelong training school of Christ. Those who would come to the throne to reign with Him, are graduates of that school.

Made to sit with Christ

The apostle Paul wrote:

> and [God] put all things in subjection under his feet, and gave him to be head over all things to the church, which is his body, the fulness of him that filleth all in all.
>
> (Ephesians 1:22–23)

Where are we? We are in Christ: everything is under *His* feet, and He has been made Head over *all things* to the Church, which is His body. The apostle then goes on to say:

> [God] raised us up with him, and made us to sit with him in the heavenly places, in Christ Jesus.
>
> (Ephesians 2:6)

Unless we learn to reign and rule with Him now, we will be unable to reign with Him in the ages to come. This is the explanation of the many hard and difficult ways the Lord leads those who will sit down with Him in His throne.

When Theodore Austin-Sparks was in his early twenties, he was greatly helped by the ministry and life of Dr F.B. Meyer. At some point in those early years, he asked if he could see him to talk about a problem he had. The arrangement was made, and Mr Sparks duly arrived at the doctor's home and was shown into his study by the mistress of the house. She apologized that Dr Meyer had been delayed, but assured Mr Sparks that he would be there shortly. With nothing to do but to wait, Mr Sparks looked around the study to see what the great man was reading and studying. Suddenly he saw on the mantelpiece a plain wooden plaque, engraved with gilded letters and the words "Look Down." Mr Sparks thought to himself, "How extraordinary! Should that not read, 'Look Up'?" It was at that point Dr F.B. Meyer entered and noticed that Mr Sparks was gazing at the plaque. He said, "I see that you are interested in those words!" "Yes," said Mr Sparks, "but should it not be, 'Look Up'?" "It is all a question of your position," replied Dr Meyer. "If you are under a problem, you have to look up; but if you are seated with Christ in heavenly places, you have to look down." Mr Sparks never forgot that interview.

Chapter 6

THE BRIDE,
THE WIFE OF THE LAMB

In the last chapter, we have seen that the sixty-six books of the Bible end with a vision of the holy city, the New Jerusalem; the bride, the wife of the Lamb. As has been pointed out, these are two very different ideas which are joined together in one. In that chapter we have already considered the first of these two matters. In this chapter we will consider the second: the bride, the wife of the Lamb.

Both of these ideas are important supporting themes in the major theme of God's Eternal Purpose. We have seen that coming to reign with the enthroned Christ is a thread that runs throughout the Bible from Genesis 1 to Revelation 22.

This second theme is as important as the first. Again we trace it from the beginning of the Bible to its end. In the first chapter of the Bible, we read:

> And God created man in his own image, in the image of God created he him; male and female created he them.
>
> (Genesis 1:27)

In the second chapter, we have a much fuller record, not only of the creation of the man but also of the woman.

> And the Lord God said, It is not good that man should be alone; I will make him a help meet for him . . . And the Lord God caused a deep sleep to fall upon the man, and he slept; and he took one of his ribs, and closed up the flesh instead thereof: and the rib, which the Lord God had taken from the man, made he a woman, and brought her unto the man. And the man said, This is now bone of my bones, and flesh of my flesh . . . Therefore shall a man leave his father and mother, and shall cleave unto his wife: and they shall be one flesh.
>
> (Genesis 2:18, 21–24)

It is to this statement that the apostle Paul specifically refers when he writes:

> This mystery is great: but I speak in regard of Christ and of the church.
>
> (Ephesians 5:32)

When we come to the last chapters of the Bible, we discover that a wedding and a marriage is joyfully and loudly proclaimed:

> Hallelujah: for the Lord our God, the Almighty, reigneth. Let us rejoice and be exceeding glad, and let us give the glory unto him: for the marriage of the Lamb is come, and his wife hath made herself ready . . . And he saith unto me, Write, Blessed are they that are bidden to the marriage supper of the Lamb . . . And he saith unto me, These are true words of God.
>
> (Revelation 19:6–9)

John further testifies:

> I saw the holy city, new Jerusalem, coming down out of heaven of God, made ready as a bride adorned for her husband.
>
> (Revelation 21:2)

What is signified by a bride and a wife? First and foremost, we should note that this is the most intimate relationship known to mankind. Carefully mark the words, "This is now bone of my bones, and flesh of my flesh . . . Therefore shall a man . . . cleave unto his wife: and they shall be one flesh." The relationship speaks of persevering, loyal, and faithful love; of union and communion; of a life that is shared; and of sensitive service.

Persevering, loyal, and faithful love

God is not interested merely in an eternal civil service, a perfect administration: knowledgeable, responsible, righteous and correct, but in practice legalistic and impersonal. It is not an everlasting bureaucracy that He seeks to establish, but He desires service that is energized by genuine love. For His eternal government, He seeks candidates who are supremely in love with Himself, and not mechanical machines who have only book knowledge.

It is surely amazing that when the Lord Jesus speaks to the church at Ephesus, He says:

> But I have this against thee, that thou didst leave thy first love. Remember therefore from whence thou art fallen, and repent and do the first works; or else I come to thee, and will remove thy lampstand [mg] out of its place, except thou repent.
>
> (Revelation 2:4–5)

This church is not like Laodicea. The Lord commends their toil, their patience, their discernment and endurance, and their rejection of error and heresy. Nevertheless, in stern words, and in spite of all that He commends, He speaks of removing the lampstand. From this we understand how supremely important to the Lord is the matter of first love.

What is *first* love? It is not "puppy" love. First love is not a question of time; it is a question of quality. When a person falls in love, normally they will travel any distance to see the loved one, put up with any difficulties involved, go to any expense, and endure all kinds of frustrating circumstances, without any murmuring and without any complaint! That is first love. That kind of love "beareth all things, believeth all things, hopeth all things, endureth all things. Love never faileth . . . " (1 Corinthians 13:7). The Lord Jesus will not be satisfied with anything less.

The quality of true love

The apostle Paul underlined the quality of true love for which the Lord is seeking when he wrote:

> If I speak with the tongues of men and of angels, but have not love, I am become sounding brass, or a clanging symbol. And if I have the gift of prophecy, and know all mysteries and all knowledge; and if I have all faith, so as to remove mountains, but have not love, I am nothing. And if I bestow all my goods to feed the poor, and if I give my body to be burned, but have not love, it profiteth me nothing.
>
> (1 Corinthians 13:1–3)

It is astounding that the estimate of the Holy Spirit is that one can have tongues and prophecy, know all mysteries and have all knowledge, possess all faith to remove mountains, give away everything to the poor, and give one's body to be burned, and without genuine love it amounts *precisely to nothing*. For this reason, we have the extraordinary combination of these two ideas in one: the holy city and the bride, the wife of the Lamb.

The Lord desires a bride who will be forever at His side because she is utterly in love with Him and devoted to Him. She is not there to obtain all the benefits, even the glory. She is there at His side, for the simple reason that she desires to be with Him.

God is Love

Everywhere we turn in the Bible, we discover that we are confronted with the love of God. God created this whole universe and the planet earth not only by His power but also out of His love. It was in love that He created man in His own image and after His own likeness. It was His love that endured the fall of man and found an answer:

> For God so loved the world, that he gave his only begotten Son, that whosoever believeth on him should not perish, but have eternal life. For God sent not the Son into the world to judge the world; but that the world should be saved through him.
>
> (John 3:16–17)

It is a profound statement that John makes when he writes: "God is love" (1 John 4:8). It is out of this fact that divine judgment comes. Evil and iniquity has to be judged if God is love. Judgment is not a contradiction of the fact that God is love, but is a principle that proceeds from it. His righteousness and justice require it. If God could simply overlook those who have wrought iniquity and evil in history, such as, for example, Nero, or Lenin, or Stalin, or Hitler, or many others, great or small, it would make His love unjust. Or take another example, can God, who is love, forget those evil and demonized men and women who perpetrated the Holocaust, as if what they did was nothing? His love for mankind in general necessitates His judgment of evil and evildoers. Only through the atoning work of the Lord Jesus can human beings, such as even these, escape coming divine judgment.

The love of God is not sentimental or emotional; it is the kind of love that, at times, is severe. The love of the Lord for His own is so strong and powerful that once those loved ones are committed to His discipline and training, He will use unusual means to bring them to the desired end. He places His greatest servants in chains, as with Joseph, with Jeremiah, and with Paul; sometimes He brings them into incredible loss, as with Job; He sets Moses, Pharoah's grandson, in the desert for forty years herding goats and sheep; and for twenty years He makes David a homeless and hunted fugitive.

The statement that "God is love" has another consequence. Since God loves, He can never be satisfied with anything less than love in return: true love always seeks love. Concerning His choice of Israel to be a special people, with a special destiny, He said:

> The Lord did not set his love upon you, nor choose you, because ye were more in number than any people; for ye were the fewest of all peoples: but because the Lord loveth you . . .
>
> (Deuteronomy 7:7–8)

Many years later, when the majority in the nation were backslidden, the Lord still declared through Jeremiah the prophet: "I have loved thee with an everlasting love: therefore with lovingkindness have I drawn thee . . . " (Jeremiah 31:3).

It is for this reason that the Lord looks for His love to be reciprocated:

> Hear, O Israel: the Lord our God is one Lord: and thou shalt love the Lord thy God with all thy heart, and with all thy soul, and with all thy might.
>
> (Deuteronomy 6:4–5)

Nothing else will ever satisfy the heart of God than those who will love Him utterly!

The Lord Jesus, the Messiah, when asked by a Pharisee lawyer a trick question, "What commandment is the first of all?", replied:

> The first is, Hear, O Israel; The Lord our God; the Lord is
> one: and thou shalt love the Lord thy God with all thy heart,
> and with all thy soul, and with all thy mind, and with all thy
> strength. The second is this, Thou shalt love thy neighbour
> as thyself. There is none other commandment greater than
> these.
>
> (Mark 12:29–31)

Matthew adds one more sentence:

> On these two commandments the whole law hangeth, and the
> prophets.
>
> (Matthew 22:40)

We should let the full meaning of what the Lord Jesus said sink
into our hearts and minds! He declared that these two commandments were not only primary and foundational, but that
the whole law and the prophets were to be explained and inter-
preted by them.

Here the Lord gave us the key to the Bible: the heart of it is
that we should love the Lord our God with everything we have
and love our neighbor as we love ourselves. If we fulfill these
two commandments, we have fulfilled the whole law and the
essential import of all prophetic ministry. It is when we properly understand these words of the Lord Jesus that we begin to
understand why the Bible ends with the bride, the wife of the
Lamb. Nothing else but loyal, persevering, and faithful love will
ever satisfy the heart of God.

Union and communion, a shared life

What is it that is signified by a bride and a wife? It is not only
this matter of loyal and utterly devoted love, it is also a question
of union and communion. When marriage was first instituted
in the garden, it was said that a man shall "leave his father and

mother, and shall cleave unto his wife: and they shall be one flesh" (Genesis 2:24). The apostle Paul wrote:

> But he that is joined unto the Lord is one spirit.
>
> (1 Corinthians 6:17)

This union with God in Christ is the consequence of being born again, of being born of the Spirit.

The Tree of Life – the eternal life of God in Christ

We can trace this matter from the first chapters of the Bible right through to the end. In the garden, there was a Tree of Life, and man was never forbidden to take the fruit of that tree, only of the fruit of the Tree of the Knowledge of Good and Evil. Those trees were literal trees, which the Lord chose to be a test of faith and obedience: faith and obedience leading to union with God, or distrust and disobedience leading to alienation from God, from His life, and from His Eternal Purpose. They also symbolize ultimate and divine truth. The Tree of Life symbolized the eternal life of God in Christ. If Adam and Eve had only taken of that tree, they would have received eternal life and, by the Spirit of God, would have been made one with Him. They would have been joined to the Lord in one spirit (consider chart iv).

Those two literal trees also symbolize two kinds of human constitution. The first, the Tree of the Knowledge of Good and Evil, represents a self-centered, self-sufficient, and self-conscious constitution; and the second, the Tree of Life, a God-centered, God-dependent, and God-conscious constitution. The Lord Jesus declared: "I am the bread of life . . . "; "I am the resurrection, and the life . . . "; and "I am the way, and the truth, and the life: no man cometh unto the Father, but by me" (John 6:35; 11:25; 14:6). In the apostle John's first letter, he wrote:

> And the witness is this, that God gave unto us eternal life, and
> this life is in his Son. He that hath the Son hath the life; he that
> hath not the Son of God hath not the life.
>
> (1 John 5:11–12)

He went on to end his letter with the words:

> And we know that the Son of God is come, and hath given us
> an understanding, that we know him that is true, and we are
> in him that is true, even in his Son Jesus Christ. This is the true
> God, and eternal life.
>
> (1 John 5:20)

It was the supreme work of the Lord Jesus to reconcile us to
God, and to make us one with Him, that we might become partakers of the divine nature (see Colossians 1:21–22; 2 Peter 1:4).
This is what it means to know and to experience Christ as the
eternal life of God.

The longing of God for fellowship

From the beginning, the Lord has longed for this union and
communion. In the Old Testament, we see this matter only in
type and figure. We have to wait until we come to the New
Testament to discover union and communion in actual experience. It comes only by the saving work of the Lord Jesus at
Calvary and by His indwelling, through the Holy Spirit, of those
He saves. Adam and Eve turned away from the Lord's purpose,
and the long, sad and sinful story began, of which we are all
part.

Throughout the Old Testament, the longing and desire of
God for fellowship is expressed and recorded. We read, for
example, that the Lord visited the garden in the cool of the day,
apparently seeking fellowship with Adam and Eve. From this
point onwards throughout the Bible, we find the Lord seeking

for those whom He could bring into fellowship with Himself.
Enoch walked with God for at least three hundred years, and it
was said of him that he "was not; for God took him" (Genesis
5:24). Apparently that was unbelievably real fellowship with the
Lord. He also brought Abraham into such a deep fellowship
with Himself that Abraham was called forever afterwards the
friend of God (see 2 Chronicles 20:7; Isaiah 41:8; James 2:23).
The Lord described Jacob as someone He loved (see Malachi
1:2), and that powerful love changed Jacob, the twister, into
Israel, the prince with God. It is recorded that he saw the face
of God and lived! It is said of Moses that the Lord spoke to him
face to face, as a man speaks to his friend (see Exodus 33:11).
The prophet and judge Samuel, with his deep understanding
of the Lord, described David as a man after God's own heart,
someone with whom God could have fellowship (see 1 Samuel
13:14). These are enough examples to demonstrate this desire
of the Lord for union and communion with those whom He
redeems.

We will come and make our abode in him

We see clearly this vital truth in the words of the Lord Jesus:

> In that day ye shall know that I am in my Father, and ye in
> me, and I in you . . . If a man love me, he will keep my word:
> and my Father will love him, and we will come unto him, and
> make our abode with him.
>
> (John 14:20, 23)

Carefully note that the Lord Jesus stated that He is in the Father,
and we are in Him, and He is in us. He declared that the Father
and the Son will come and make their home in us. It is clear from
the context that it is the Holy Spirit who makes this union and
communion a living reality. Thus, the triune God is involved in
the realization of this work.

The Lord Jesus commanded those whom He has saved by His grace: "Abide in me, and I in you." He went on to say:

> I am the vine, ye are the branches: He that abideth in me, and I in him, the same beareth much fruit: for apart from me ye can do nothing.
>
> (John 15:4–5)

Here again we have this matter of union and communion. We should note those stark words: "Apart from me ye can do nothing." If they were fully understood, much of our Christian life, of our church life, of our service, and our work for the Lord would be seen to be self-manufactured, amounting to nothing.

Those who are born of God are placed by the Father in Christ. That is their position. We are not commanded to strive or to struggle to be in Him, or by stint of devotion and zeal to attain to such a position. God has *already placed us in Him* and, incredibly, *has placed Him in us*. We are to abide, or to remain, where God has placed us. This truth is the key to so much in the New Testament. We discover that in Christ God has given everything of Himself; and when Christ steps into a human being, He brings the infinite fullness of God into that person. O for eyes to see this truth in reality, and to experience it in practice! Dear reader, a simple study of the phrases "in Christ" and "Christ in you" could be life changing!

Union with God and communion

In His high-priestly prayer the Lord Jesus prayed:

> And the glory which thou hast given me I have given unto them; that they may be one, even as we are one; I in them, and thou in me, that they may be perfected into one . . .
>
> (John 17:22–23)

These words cause our finite minds to stagger. Is it possible that human beings such as we can be brought into such a union with God? The answer is simple. It is yes! If we have been born anew, that is our eternal position, and it does not depend on us, but on God Himself. He has positioned us *in Christ*. If we are in Christ, then *Christ is in us*, with all the potential necessary for us to reach His goal.

From this union with Christ comes communion; and from both union and communion, sensitive service is born. What is communion? Paul concludes his second letter to the Corinthians with the words:

> The grace of the Lord Jesus Christ, and the love of God, and the communion of the Holy Spirit, be with you all.
>
> (2 Corinthians 13:14)

The Greek word *koinonia*, translated in English by the word "communion," means simply to have something in common: fellowship, sharing, or participation. He uses the same word when he writes:

> The cup of blessing which we bless, is it not a communion of the blood of Christ? The bread which we break, is it not a communion of the body of Christ? seeing that we, who are many, are one bread, one body: for we all partake of the one bread.
>
> (1 Corinthians 10:16–17)

It is one loaf that is shared; it is a shared cup. Again, the Holy Spirit uses the same word when Paul writes:

> God is faithful, through whom ye were called into the fellowship of his Son Jesus Christ our Lord.
>
> (1 Corinthians 1:9)

God calls us into a participation in the Lord Jesus. We are members of Christ and members one of another. It is the life and destiny of the Lord Jesus which we share. It is the fellowship or communion of His Son.

What then is *communion?* We who are saved by the grace of God are called to share the life of the Lord Jesus, to share His vision, to share His interests, and, unbelievably, to share His destiny. For we are called to be heirs of God and joint heirs with the Messiah (see Romans 8:17). Concerning this subject Paul declares: "being justified by his grace, we might be made heirs according to the hope of eternal life" (Titus 3:7). This is further confirmed by James when he writes:

> Hearken, my beloved brethren; did not God choose them that are poor as to the world to be rich in faith, and heirs of the kingdom which he promised to them that love him?
>
> (James 2:5)

Our calling is not only to be saved but to share the reign of our Lord Jesus in the ages to come. So great is the love of God that He desires those whom He saves to be His heirs, and to be joint heirs with His Son. This is the high calling with which we are called.

Spiritually sensitive service

Sensitive service is born out of this union and communion with the Messiah, and it is something for which the Lord seeks, and upon which He places great value. The Lord Jesus wants a bride, a wife, who can share with Him in the fulfillment of His will in the ages to come. It is not a Hollywood star for which He seeks: beautiful looks, beautiful hair, beautiful eyes, beautiful figure, and nothing between the ears! He is not seeking someone who can sit on His throne and "look pretty." He desires a bride who not only wants to be with Him because she loves Him, but a bride who can, with Him, govern a new heaven and a new earth with spiritual intelligence and sensitive service.

What do I mean by "sensitive service"? I mean the kind of service that above all has a heart of love for the Lord and for others. So often, divine love is the missing element in our work and service. This is precisely what the Lord meant when He spoke of leaving one's first love. Then our service and work can become icily correct, dutiful, conscientious, sound, but with no heart. The Lord Jesus said to Peter, "Do you love Me more than these?" And went on to say, "Tend My lambs . . . shepherd My sheep . . . tend My sheep" (see John 21:15–27). All that service and work has to come from our love for the Lord, otherwise it amounts to nothing. That is the divine verdict!

We have all suffered at some time or another from Christians, or Christian workers, or elders, or shepherds, or pastors, or leaders whose service is sound and correct, but is lacking that absolutely essential element of divine love. How all of us who are called to serve, need to have a continuous baptism of the love of God. It is out of that continuously renewed love in our hearts that *sensitive* service is produced. That kind of love will always keep us sensitive to the Lord in our service and in our work. At any given moment He can challenge us or correct us and bring us back into line with Himself, and thus keep us in "first love."

Chapter 7

THE NECESSITY OF SPIRITUAL CHARACTER

Amazingly, there are only three materials out of which the holy city, the new Jerusalem, and the bride, the wife of the Lamb, are produced. Here again we are faced with something unique. No capital city has ever been built out of gold, precious stone, and pearl. There may be much gold, many precious stones, and pearls within such a city; but we search in vain throughout the long history of the nations to find a single city that has been produced solely out of these three materials.

It also hardly needs to be stated that there has never been a bride or a wife who was formed out of gold, precious stone, and pearl! One could find many instances of such brides, or wives, who were bedecked, or even loaded, with such precious treasure, but never a single incidence of one of them being formed out of those materials! What then is the significance of this seemingly bizarre fact?

In the extraordinary vision with which God concludes the revelation of His heart and mind in the Bible, I have repeatedly emphasized that we have two quite different ideas combined into one: a city and a bride. We have concentrated on this matter in the last two chapters. Now we have to face another astonishing truth. *These three materials signify the essential necessity of spiritual character.* There can be no city of God, and no bride of Christ, without such character!

Where thy treasure is, there will thy heart be also

It is a sobering fact that we can carry nothing with us into eternity but that which God works in us. Job said: "Naked came I out of my mother's womb, and naked shall I return thither . . . " (Job 1:21). The preacher also states the same truth when he said:

> As he came forth from his mother's womb, naked shall he go again as he came, and shall take nothing for his labor, which he may carry away in his hand.
>
> (Ecclesiastes 5:15)

The apostle Paul confirms it with the words: "for we brought nothing into the world, for neither can we carry anything out" (1 Timothy 6:7). It matters not how much money we have made, or how extensive is the business empire we have built, or how much property we own, or how successful is our career, or how many degrees or titles we may have; we can carry none of it into eternity! We cannot even take the clothes in which we are buried or the personal jewelry we wear.

I remember many years ago listening to a story that Lindsay Glegg recounted. He was a well-known evangelist in his time. He said that when the first edition of the famous *Sacred Songs and Solos* was published, a mistake of one letter was found in a well-known and greatly loved hymn, which apparently the proofreaders had missed. The famous hymn was "Guide Me, O Thou Great Jehovah" and, instead of reading, "land me safe on Canaan's side," it read, "land *my* safe on Canaan's side." Lindsay Glegg said that the edition had to be withdrawn. He went on to say, "Many a person would love their safe to be landed on Canaan's side, but it will never happen!" How little time we all give to the work of the Holy Spirit in us, and how much time we all focus on those things which are temporal and transient, none of which we can carry into eternity.

Only that which God works in us can produce eternal value.

> I know that, whatsoever God doeth, it shall be for ever: nothing can be put to it, nor anything taken from it; and God hath done it . . .
>
> (Ecclesiastes 3:14)

This is what gold, precious stone, and pearl symbolize and signify: the eternal work of the Lord in a saved human being. The Lord Jesus stated it simply:

> Lay not up for yourselves treasures upon the earth, where moth and rust consume, and where thieves break through and steal: but lay up for yourselves treasures in heaven, where neither moth nor rust doth consume, and where thieves do not break through nor steal: for where thy treasure is, there will thy heart be also.
>
> (Matthew 6:19–21)

The Lord seeks to create spiritual character in every child of His. In practice, it is the Holy Spirit who produces this "treasure in heaven." He forms heavenly and spiritual gold, precious stone, and pearl. It is out of this eternal treasure that the city of God and the bride of Christ are produced.

It is obvious that to reign with Christ, spiritual character is an essential necessity. It is also as obvious that to be the bride of Christ, the wife of the Lamb, spiritual character is an indispensable requirement. Unbelievable as it may seem, God places this treasure of gold, precious stone, and pearl in earthen vessels (see 2 Corinthians 4:7–10). From this treasure, which is Christ in us, He then works to produce both the city and the bride. The apostle Paul wrote:

> to whom God was pleased to make known what is the riches of the glory of this mystery among the Gentiles, which is Christ in you, the hope of glory . . .
>
> (Colossians 1:27)

This gold, this precious stone, and this pearl are all aspects of Christ and symbolize the spiritual character He produces in His child. Such character is alone the material for coming glory.

Gold, the nature and life of Christ

Godly and spiritual Bible teachers have always pointed to the fact that *gold* in the Bible symbolizes the life and nature of Christ. In my estimation, that is incontrovertible. Any serious Bible student will know that the mercy seat, made of pure gold in both the tabernacle and the temple, is a type or symbol of the Messiah. The Lord says:

> And there I will meet with thee, and I will commune with thee from above the mercy-seat, from between the two cherubim which are upon the ark of the testimony, of all things which I will give thee in commandment unto the children of Israel.
>
> (Exodus 25:22, cf. Romans 3:25; Hebrews 4:16)

The ark of the covenant, also overlaid with gold, and the testimony within it, of the unbroken law, the golden pot of manna, and Aaron's rod that budded, all speak of the Lord Jesus: His life, His nature, and His finished work. It is also true, in fact, of the lampstand all of gold, of the golden altar of incense, and of the golden table of shewbread: all speak of the Lord Jesus.

It is interesting to note that when the wise men, the magi, came to Bethlehem to find the infant King, the promised

Messiah, it is recorded: "they fell down and worshipped him; and opening their treasures, they offered unto him gifts, gold and frankincense and myrrh" (Matthew 2:11). The frankincense was part of the especial holy incense used on the golden altar, which signified the intercessory work of Christ; the myrrh signified His atoning death, by which He won our salvation; and the gold speaks of the eternal life of God, which Christ manifested and has given to those who trust in Him.

We are told in the second chapter of the Bible that we shall find gold if we follow the course of the river. It has to be discovered and refined before it can be fashioned and used. At the end of the Bible, we find that both God's capital city and the bride of Christ are formed out of pure gold. It has been refined to a degree that no gold has ever been refined, for it is as transparent as glass or crystal. This is unusual and astonishing, for it speaks of a degree of refinement that is unknown to any goldsmith.

This gold speaks of the life of the Lord Jesus in those whom He saves: He is the life of God in us. In many ways, it is summed up in the words of the Messiah: "I counsel thee to buy of me gold refined by fire, that thou mayest become rich . . . " (Revelation 3:18). We should note carefully the counsel of the Lord Jesus. If He is seeking to advise us, then we need to wake up and carefully attend to exactly what is His concern. The fact that He counsels us to buy gold of Him means that we may not have it. This advice was to a church that believed it was rich, had acquired riches, and had need of nothing. They were born of God, saved by His grace, and yet according to the Lord they were miserable, poor, and naked. It is always a sign of spiritual lukewarmness and apathy when we believe we have something we do not actually possess. On the other hand, it is a sign of revival and renewal when we begin to recognize our spiritual poverty, and, awakened by Him, we begin to hear and obey His counsel.

We need His resurrection life and power in fullness, for it is within His resurrection that we discover the gold! He counsels us to *buy of Him* gold refined by fire. We may well ask, is not His salvation and His life given to us without any attached price? The answer is straightforward: they are given through the free grace of God and not through our works. Why then do we need to *buy* this gold? The simple answer is that for the formation of spiritual character there is a cost to be borne. God will give us freely as much *gold* as we can receive, but there is a price to pay! That price is deep and costly genuine experience.

It is gold *refined by fire*. Certainly what we receive of the Lord Jesus is obtained through His agony at Calvary. It is the gold of His life, refined by His incredible suffering. Yet for those who would *buy* this gold, there is also a refining process through which they must pass. Job testifies to this when he declared:

> But he knoweth the way that I take;
> When he hath tried me, I shall come forth as gold.
>
> (Job 23:10)

When I lived for a few years in Egypt, I asked two old missionaries, who had spent a lifetime there, about the process of the refinement of gold and silver. In those days, the age-old methods were still practiced. They said that the goldsmith or silversmith placed the molten gold or silver in a crucible over a fire and watched it until he could clearly see his face. At that point he knew that the impurities had been refined out of it, and he would remove it from the fire. If he left it any longer, it could damage the quality of the gold or silver.

This is certainly true of what the Lord does with us. He is waiting to see clearly His image or His likeness in us.

> The refining pot is for silver, and the furnace for gold;
> But the Lord trieth the hearts.
>
> (Proverbs 17:3)

This truth is stated again in Malachi:

> But who can abide the day of his coming? and who shall stand when he appeareth? for he is like a refiner's fire . . . and he will sit as a refiner and purifier of silver, and he will purify the sons of Levi, and refine them as gold and silver; and they shall offer unto the Lord offerings in righteousness.
>
> (Malachi 3:2–3)

We see this refining process of the Spirit of God described in the words of John the Baptist:

> "As for me, I baptize you with water for repentance, but He who is coming after me is mightier than I, and I am not fit to remove His sandals: He will baptize you with the Holy Spirit and fire. His winnowing fork is in His hand, and He will thoroughly clear His threshing floor; and He will gather His wheat into the barn, but He will burn up the chaff with unquenchable fire."
>
> (Matthew 3:11–12 NASB)

This refining work of the Holy Spirit is not always emphasized; the emphasis is on His empowering and indwelling work. Burning up the chaff in our lives is not a popular theme, but it is essential. John the Baptist exemplified this aspect when he said: "He must increase, but I must decrease" (John 3:30). It is always a costly experience to be reduced, but the gain is always eternal. The more there is of Christ in us, the more there is that can be and will be glorified!

The best commentary on this refining process is contained in the testimony of the apostle Paul:

> Howbeit what things were gain to me, these have I counted loss for Christ. Yea verily, and I count all things to be loss for the excellency of the knowledge of Christ Jesus my Lord: for

whom I suffered the loss of all things, and do count them but
refuse, that I may gain Christ, and be found in him, not having
a righteousness of mine own, even that which is of the law, but
that which is through faith in Christ, the righteousness which
is from God by faith: that I may know him, and the power of
his resurrection, and the fellowship of his sufferings, becoming
conformed unto his death . . .

(Philippians 3:7–10)

Only by the gold of His life and nature can the bride of Christ,
the wife of the Lamb, and the city of God be produced. It is
summed up in a phrase that the apostle Paul used in his testimony: "that I may gain Christ." What did he mean when he
spoke of "gaining Christ"? After all, Christ is God's unspeakable
gift to us: He is given to us in all His fullness through the grace
of God alone. However, *we have to possess* what is freely given
to us in Christ. We have to lay hold on that for which He laid
hold on us! We need to buy of Him gold refined by fire. Samuel
Rutherford, the old Puritan divine, said: "Men want Christ
cheap. They want Him without the cross, but the price will not
come down."

Precious stones, the excellencies and beauties of Christ

The second material out of which the bride of the Messiah
and the city of God are produced is precious stone. All twelve
foundations of this city and the whole wall are formed out of
it. Precious stone is formed by intense heat and pressure, in the
dark places of the earth. It has to be discovered, mined, cut, and
polished before it can become an object of beauty and of art-
istry. Once again, we have to "follow the river of life" to discover it. Precious stone is something that is produced by the life
of Christ in us.

What is symbolized by precious stone? Godly Bible teachers and students of the Word of God have taught us that it is the glories, the excellencies, and the beauties of the Lord Jesus that are represented by it. Every time a child of God catches a glimpse of these in another believer, he or she is awestruck and can only worship the Lord for the work He has done. Anyone who has seen genuine precious gemstones will understand the beauty and excellence which they radiate; they can captivate the onlooker!

These qualities of Christ did not come easily or cheaply to Him as a man. He was described as "despised, and rejected of men; a man of sorrows, and acquainted with grief" (Isaiah 53:3). The writer of the Hebrew letter wrote: "though he was a Son, yet learned obedience by the things which he suffered" (5:8). Even the Lord Jesus experienced that which is signified by the "cutting" and the "polishing" of precious stone! The end result was incredible, for like the most precious of gemstones He radiated the light, the life, and the love of God. The apostle John put this into words when he wrote: "and we saw His glory, glory as of the only begotten from the Father, full of grace and truth" (John 1:14 NASB).

This precious stone, out of which the bride of Christ and the city of God are formed, signifies spiritual character. There is no substitute for it. Wood, hay, and stubble are the common, natural qualities of our flesh. It is what we generate and produce naturally. So often, much of our Christian life and service is self-manufactured. It is wood, hay, and stubble, even though fashioned at times into something that appears to be the real thing. It is also true of so much church life (see 1 Corinthians 3:11–15). Precious stone is formed out of the life of Christ within the believer and comes, once again, through costly experience. Wood, hay, and stubble are temporal; precious stone is eternal. There are, however, few believers ready to bear the cost of the deep dealings of God, which alone can produce this character.

The apostle Paul, in his testimony, speaks of counting all things to be loss for the excellency of the knowledge of Christ Jesus the Lord. He was not talking about head knowledge, but knowing inwardly, and personally, the excellency of the Messiah. The apostle Peter writes: "that ye may show forth the excellencies of him who called you out of darkness into his marvellous light" (1 Peter 2:9). Anyone who has beheld the beauty of the Lord, the excellency of the Lord, in another believer knows how heart warming is such an experience. Indeed, such believers have an impact upon all who touch them, whether saved or unsaved. Where such beauty and excellency is radiated, it is the "precious stone" of the life of Christ. It is the genuine evidence of spiritual character.

Pearl, the fellowship of His sufferings

The third material out of which alone the city of God and the bride of Christ are formed, is pearl. We are told that each of the twelve gates consists of one single pearl. We should note that this is a pearl far larger than anyone has ever seen on this earth. I myself have seen some of the pearls which the Empress Dowager of the Ching Dynasty wore. They were the size of pigeon eggs. As large as they were, they were nothing in comparison to the pearls of the twelve gates.

The twelve single pearls which constitute the twelve gates, are enormous! At the heart of each of these huge pearls is a piece of worthless grit or debris: a foreign substance which has found its way into the clam. It would have been the amazing energy within the life of the clam which produced such priceless pearls through coating the grit again and again. The clam was seeking, with all its power, to eject the intruding and alien debris, or at least to make it easier to accept. Whatever does all this signify?

In ancient walled cities, gates were of tremendous significance. They were the only means of access and of exit. The gates, especially in Israel, were the place where judgment was given and government administered. The elders "sat in the gates." Thus we understand that the Lord is seeking to produce the kind of spiritual character which results in spiritual authority and the ability to govern. The highest places in His government will be filled by those whom these pearls represent. All the business, all the work, and all the intercourse of the city pass through those gates.

There is nothing sentimental or romantic about the production of a pearl. An alien substance has entered the mollusc and irritated it, and it has resulted in a pearl. This speaks of a kind of suffering not given to everyone, but only to those who are willing to go the whole way with the Lord. It is summed up in the words: "that I may know him, and the power of his resurrection, and the fellowship of his sufferings . . ." (Philippians 3:10). This fellowship, this communion, this sharing of His sufferings, leads to the formation of these twelve single pearls.

The production of pearl – My grace is sufficient for thee

Paul speaks mysteriously in his letter to the Colossians when he says:

> Now I rejoice in my sufferings for your sake, and fill up on my part that which is lacking of the afflictions of Christ in my flesh for his body's sake, which is the church . . .
>
> (Colossians 1:24)

However, there is a clarity in the words which he wrote:

> And by reason of the exceeding greatness of the revelations, that I should not be exalted overmuch, there was given to me a thorn in the flesh, a messenger of Satan to buffet me, that I should not be exalted overmuch. Concerning this thing, I

besought the Lord thrice, that it might depart from me. And he hath said unto me, My grace is sufficient for thee: for my power is made perfect in weakness. Most gladly therefore will I rather glory in my weaknesses, that the power of Christ may rest upon me. Wherefore I take pleasure in weaknesses, in injuries, in necessities, in persecutions, in distresses, for Christ's sake: for when I am weak, then am I strong.

(2 Corinthians 12:7–10)

We should note that Paul was given what he called "a thorn in the flesh." Here is the foreign substance, the grit! He actually called this thorn "a messenger of Satan to buffet me," or to pummel me. He considered that it was the destruction of his ministry and spiritual life, and he had sought the Lord three times to remove it when he wrote this letter. On each of those occasions the Lord had answered him with the same words, "My grace is sufficient for thee." This grace was the coating of the foreign substance that had entered his experience. It resulted in the formation of a pearl of great price, and an immensely precious and valuable ministry to the Church.

A parable of jade

Many years ago, in the drawing room of the home of a Swedish sister, who became "Auntie Dagmar" to both myself and my sister, I listened, entranced, as an old missionary spoke. It was Mildred Cable of the China Inland Mission. She and her two companions, Francesca and Evangeline French, were known as "the trio." They became renowned for their labors: they traversed the whole area of the Gobi desert, of Inner Mongolia, and Northwest China, preaching the gospel. They often stayed with Auntie Dagmar when they were in Britain.

On this occasion, Mildred Cable was talking about jade. Some years later she put all of it into writing, in a booklet entitled "A Parable of Jade." She told of how the rough boulders were transported by camel caravan from Chinese Turkestan to Beijing. There they were sold in the jade market to jade smiths. She recounted how sometimes these rough pieces of jade had a flaw, which could have made them useless. The jade smith who had bought the uncut boulders would never be in a hurry. It was the flaw that was the heart of the problem, and he needed wisdom. At different times he would take them down from a shelf, unwrap the cloth around them, and contemplate them, whilst drinking Chinese tea. His problem was how to handle the work. Sometimes it took months and, on occasion, even years until he discovered what he should do. Once the master jade craftsman had formed the idea of how to handle it, he would turn the flaw into the focal point of the work he was producing. It was the art of a master craftsman.

Many times I have seen the result of such craftsmanship. The flaw has become a brown-black bee on a white peony flower, or a brown frog on a green lotus leaf, or a bird on a branch. The amazing thing is that the flaw has now become the focal point of the beauty of the work. Although jade is not pearl, we see in this matter the same principle: something that is foreign, such as grit or a flaw, that seemingly would render the whole piece worthless, has become the heart of a work of art. The Lord Jesus is such a master craftsman and master artist when it comes to producing the kind of character that in the end will be an essential and integral part of the city.

Amy Carmichael of Dohnavur

There are two servants of God, out of many, who illustrate the truth expressed in these pearls. One of those servants of God is Amy Carmichael of Dohnavur in southern India.

Amy Carmichael had received a calling from God to India and had obeyed the call, and through the Lord had built up an incredible work. It was a work of redemption: saving baby girls from a life of prostitution, mainly in temples, and providing them with a loving and caring home, amid Christian surroundings.

The work was growing, and she traveled a number of miles, with other co-workers, to view some premises that could have become an extension of the work. When they arrived, the man with the key was not there. They waited and waited until the tropical dusk suddenly fell. Then he arrived. They all stood back out of respect to let Amy Carmichael enter first. Unknown to all of them, a coolie had dug a deep trench just inside the gate. It was a mistake. No one ever found out why that trench was dug. Amy Carmichael fell into the trench and suffered very badly broken and fractured bones. Tenderly they lifted her into the jeep for the journey back over rough, unmade roads. In the hospital, they attended to her, and she was taken back to Dohnavur.

After six months, she wrote a book entitled *Rose from Brier*, in which she spoke of the lessons she had learnt from her accident, and which she felt would be of comfort and help to others with a similar experience to hers. Amy Carmichael apologized in it for the fact that *her* being laid aside was for so short a time; "I will only be on my back for a few months," she said. In fact, she would never walk again. Amy Carmichael's worldwide ministry had begun with that fall. It was a pearl of unbelievable quality that was being formed. Over the years, whenever I needed to help someone in inexplicable suffering or circumstances, the only ministry, I discovered, which spoke to the heart of that person was the ministry of Amy Carmichael. It was "deep calling unto deep."

Fannie Crosby – the blind hymn writer

The other servant of God is Fannie Crosby, the great hymn writer of the nineteenth century. She was a little girl when she suffered a not very serious eye infection. A doctor was called, and he, inadvertently, administered to her not the eye solution she needed but an acid. The eyes of Fannie Crosby were destroyed. She never saw again. Instead she saw the Lord with the eyes of her heart, and she ministered with her joyful hymns to millions of believers, then and ever since. It was a pearl of great price that was being formed.

The all-important question of spiritual character

This question of spiritual character is all important to the Lord. It is after all the outworking of our "so great salvation." Where there is a willing heart, He will go to enormous lengths to produce this kind of character. It is interesting to note that the apostle Paul was greatly burdened concerning the formation of such spiritual character in those he had led to the Lord Jesus. He expressed it in a letter. He wrote:

> My little children, of whom I am again in travail until Christ be formed in you . . .
>
> (Galatians 4:19)

The Greek word translated by the English "travail" denotes the agonizing pain of childbirth: no small or trivial pain! This indicates a deep work of the Spirit in the apostle. He was so united to the Lord, and so sensitive to Him, that a travail such as this could be conceived within his own spirit.

Note also the word "again." It is clear that the apostle had already been in travail for their salvation. Now he was again in travail that Christ be formed in them. It is an arresting statement, and quite out of sorts with so much modern Christianity. What does Paul mean: "that Christ be formed in you"? Were they not born again? Was Christ not already dwelling in them? The answer is, yes, they were born of God and had received Christ. It was the question of spiritual growth, of spiritual character, that so burdened the apostle. This was no small matter, for it was then, and is now, related to God's Eternal Purpose.

We have only one short life to live, which lasts, on average, a short seventy years! Compared with eternity, it is a pin prick. In that life, the Lord has to arrange our circumstances, convict us of sin, lead us to His salvation, bring about our spiritual birth, and then change us into the likeness of the Lord Jesus. In those quickly passing years, He has to produce spiritual character. For the most part, we are not the most cooperative of people and give Him endless trouble. Gold, precious stone, and pearl are not instantly produced commodities. There are no short cuts in their formation. The truth is stark and, for many, hard to digest, but there are no alternatives or substitutes. Spiritual character is spiritual character, and nothing else will satisfy God.

Chapter 8

THE ENTHRONED LAMB

The last book of the Bible, entitled "The Revelation of John" or the Apocalypse, as we would expect, is the summing up of everything in the previous sixty-five books. The plain fact is that it is impossible to understand the imagery and figures used in this book without some familiarity, for example, with Ezekiel, Daniel, and Zechariah, to name just a few books. The Revelation of John is the top stone in Holy Scripture of the unveiling of God's heart and mind to mankind.

The key to the book is found in its first sentence: the revelation of Jesus the Messiah (see Revelation 1:1). It is therefore all centered in Christ: in His person, in His finished work, in His triumph and glory, and in those who belong to Him. Such is the importance of this revelation that a blessing is pronounced in the first sentences of the opening chapter on those who read it, and who hear it with the ear of their spirit, and who keep the things that are written within it. In the final chapter, this blessing is confirmed and underlined (see Revelation 1:3; 22:7).

As in Genesis we have "all the beginnings," so in Revelation we have all the conclusions; the final issues or outcome of everything. The Greek word *apokalupsis,* translated by the English word "revelation," means simply "to take the cover off"; hence, the other title of this book, the Apocalypse. It is the unveiling of God's Eternal Purpose centered in the person of the Lord Jesus, and in those whom He saves. Even the future liberation of the natural creation is related to the redemption of God and His Eternal Purpose (see Romans 8:18–24). In the light of that unveiling of God's purpose for the Messiah, we have the "uncovering" of the real nature of Satan, of his hierarchy, and of their rebellion; the "uncovering" of fallen man and the depths to which he can sink when energized by Satan; and the "uncovering" of the utterly futile agenda of the nations without God, summed up in "Babylon the Great."

There are at least four different interpretations of this book, which tend to confuse many who seek to study it. Even sound Bible teachers have problems with these conflicting interpretations. Indeed, not a few Christians avoid reading the book altogether, either because they are confused or because they find it depressingly negative! In the end, however, it is a question of what one is seeking in this book. If one looks for Satan, for demons, for beasts, for a false prophet, for a prostitute church, for martyrdom and death, and for catastrophic judgments, one will find them all there in full measure. If, however, one is looking for the triumphant and risen Christ, enthroned in glory, for the city of God, the new Jerusalem, for the bride of Christ, the wife of the Lamb, for a new heaven and a new earth wherein dwells righteousness, for the final triumph of the saints, one will also find it all there in this book.

One needs to remember that the apostle John was himself in extremely negative and depressing circumstances when this revelation was given to him. He was a Roman prisoner in a forced labor camp, alienated from all those whom he loved and with whom he had been in the closest fellowship. What he saw was not dark or depressing, but, for him, a vision of coming freedom and glory! For us, therefore, it should also be a revelation of the total authority and power of the risen Messiah, whatever our present conditions and afflictions might be. It is not my intention, however, to expound the book of Revelation, and I must leave that to those more able and more qualified to do it. My aim in this chapter is to emphasize the realization and securing of God's Eternal Purpose in the Messiah, as we discover it in this book.

It is a stunning vision that is given to us in the fourth and fifth chapters of Revelation. John saw at the center of heaven, and therefore of all creation, a rainbow-encircled throne, with the brilliance of an emerald. Upon that seat of all Sovereignty and Authority was One enthroned, who radiated the luminous brightness of precious stone. It was the Almighty and living God. Round about the throne were twenty-four enthroned elders, seemingly twelve from the Old Covenant and twelve from the New. We discover again this figure of twenty-four in the city of God: there are twelve patriarchs and twelve apostles (see Revelation 4:4; 21:12, 14). In the midst, before the throne, were four living creatures. These composite beings seem to represent the whole natural creation of God, including man (see Revelation 4:6–11).

As John watched this incredible scene, he saw that the enthroned One in the midst had in His right hand a scroll sealed with seven seals. Then he heard a strong angelic voice proclaiming: "Who is worthy to open the scroll [mg] and to break its seals?" (see Revelation 5:2 NASB). An absolute silence followed, without any movement. John understood the significance of that scroll and its seals, and began to cry uncontrollably. One of the elders then said to him:

> "Stop weeping; behold, the Lion that is from the tribe of Judah, the Root of David, has overcome so as to open the scroll [mg] and its seven seals."
>
> (Revelation 5:5 NASB)

Through his tears, John sought to see this Lion from the tribe of Judah, this Root of David. Instead he saw, in the midst of the throne of God, a little Lamb standing, as though it had just been slain. The Greek word *arnion*, translated by the English word "lamb," is a diminutive and means "a little lamb." The impact on John is better understood if we translate it: "he saw in the midst of the throne . . . a little lamb as slaughtered." The title of the Messiah "the Lion of Judah," with all its majesty, strength, and power, and the title "the Root of David" encompass the entire Old Testament and are the key to Jewish history and destiny. John saw that the little slaughtered Lamb was in fact the Lion of Judah and the Root of David.

Beholding this little slaughtered Lamb, he saw Him take the scroll out of the right hand of the enthroned One. Then the four living creatures and the twenty-four elders fell down before the little Lamb and broke into song and worship:

> "Worthy are You to take the scroll [mg] and to break its seals; for You were slain, and purchased for God with Your blood men from every tribe and tongue and people and nation. You have made them to be a kingdom and priests to our God; and they will reign upon the earth."
>
> (Revelation 5:9–10 NASB)

As he continued to watch, he heard the voices of myriads upon myriads of angels, saying:

> "Worthy is the Lamb that was slain to receive power and riches and wisdom and might and honor and glory and blessing."
>
> (Revelation 5:12 NASB)

With that proclamation, he heard every created thing joining in and saying:

> "To Him who sits on the throne, and to the Lamb, be blessing and honor and glory and dominion forever and ever."
>
> (Revelation 5:13 NASB)

Then the four living creatures said "Amen," and the twenty-four elders fell down and worshiped! All knew that God had secured the fulfillment of His Eternal Purpose, and they could do no other than prostrate themselves in worship before Him.

The sealed scroll, the Eternal Purpose of God

John had clearly understood the significance of the scroll sealed with seven seals. In the ancient Jewish world, when a will or testament was drawn up, it was written on a scroll and sealed with seals. He had realized that the living God, the Almighty, did not need to leave a will or a testament, as if He would die! Thus John understood that the scroll and its seals symbolized the whole purpose of God. He was mortified that not a single angel or elder, or for that matter anyone else, could respond to the question of the angel, "Who is worthy?", and he burst into tears. The fulfillment of the whole Eternal Purpose of God was on hold: it was paralyzed. When he was told that the Lion of Judah had overcome to open the scroll, it made sense. It was Jesus the Messiah, of the tribe of Judah and of the royal house, the house of David. The whole of Jewish history, which began with Abraham, and the promise which God had made to him that a great and unique nation would come out of his loins and, furthermore, that in him all the nations of the earth would be blessed, had been fulfilled (see Genesis 12:1–3).

It had been fulfilled not by the strength and power and majesty of the Lion, but through a little Lamb as slaughtered at Calvary. This supreme work of Jesus, the long-promised Messianic king, the king of Israel, is the foundation upon which God realizes and secures His whole purpose. The crucified Messiah, Christ crucified, is the power of God to save both Jew and Gentile; and the power and majesty of the Lion of Judah had been manifested in and through the little Lamb as slain. It is not possible to make a dichotomy between the Lion of Judah, the Root of David, and the little Lamb, as if they were two incompatible and totally different roles. The Lion of Judah *is* "the little Lamb as slain."

It is incredible to hear the words of worship that were sung as a result of the Lamb taking the scroll:

"Worthy are You to take the scroll, and to break its seals; for You were slain, and purchased for God with Your blood men from every tribe and tongue and people and nation."

The promise of God to Abraham is being fulfilled through the finished work of the Lamb. From every part of the earth, men and women of all races, all cultures, all languages, and all colors are being saved. Nor has God forgotten His promise concerning the Jewish people. The little Lamb is, after all, the Lion of the tribe of Judah and the Root of David. As the apostle Paul stated it:

As touching the gospel, they are enemies for your sake [i.e. the true Church], but as touching the election, they are beloved for the patriarchs' sake, for the gifts and the calling of God are irrevocable.

(Romans 11:28–29)

It is of great importance to understand what John means in Revelation 5:10 when he writes, "You have made them to be a kingdom and priests to our God; and they will reign upon the earth." The Greek word *basileia*, translated by the English word "kingdom," means "royal dominion or kingdom." We should, however, note that it is followed by the statement "and they will reign upon the earth." It is not merely a matter of being ruled over by the king, but of reigning with Him; it is a question of kingship. Here we are again face to face with God's Eternal Purpose. We have been purchased by the blood of the Lamb to be a royal dominion, a kingdom, a kingship, and priests to our God.

The revelation of the enthroned Lamb

From this amazing revelation of the enthroned Lamb, everything in this book proceeds. The Messiah, Christ, begins from this point onwards to break one seal after another, with the most powerful and dramatic consequences. Then out of the seventh seal come seven trumpets, and out of the seventh trumpet come seven bowls, until we see the holy city, the New Jerusalem, coming down out of heaven from God, made ready as a bride adorned for her husband.

The one thing that is absolutely clear throughout the whole of this book is the total victory of the Lion of Judah, the little Lamb. It seems clear, at least to me, that the vision we have in the fourth and fifth chapters of Revelation is the reign of the Lord Jesus which began at His ascension to the right hand of God. He had said before that event: "All authority hath been given unto me in heaven and on earth" (Matthew 28:18). Throughout all the war recorded in this book, both on earth and in heaven, the intense conflict, the martyrdom of true believers, and the catastrophic judgments of God, *the Lamb is enthroned and triumphant*. He has won and is waiting until the Father makes all His enemies His footstool. Furthermore, He is not idle, but rules: the rod of His strength goes forth out of Zion, and He rules in the midst of His enemies (see Psalm 110:1–2; cf. Acts 2:33–36).

He rules in the midst of His enemies

"He rules in the midst of His enemies" is a perfect description of the role of the Lamb in the first twenty chapters of Revelation. The continuous battle described in those chapters does not *precede* the triumph and reign of the Messiah but, rather, *proceeds* from it. It is as if the enemy can no longer touch the Lord Jesus, or change the Father's predestined purpose and plan for Him. Therefore he seeks to touch those on the earth redeemed by

Him and to frustrate the work of the Holy Spirit in them. His strategy is to redirect the children of God into other paths; to deflect them from the goal of their salvation; to spoil them or to rob them by one means or another; and to trap them in spiritual infancy, sidetracking them from their high calling.

We see the evidence of this in the long history of the Church. The Lord Jesus declared: "upon this rock I will build my church, and the gates of hell shall not prevail against it" (Matthew 16:18 KJV). The building of the Church by the Lord Jesus has been an amazing story of conflict, raging back and forth. Many times it has seemed that the powers of darkness and of death have prevailed. The fact that the true Church is still very much alive in the twenty-first century is due to the invincible building work of the Lord Jesus. Again and again, when "the Church" has become lifeless, at times a nest of demons, and often a cruel and tyrannical system persecuting faithful believers, the Lord Jesus by the Holy Spirit has initiated powerful movements that have again set forward His building work. Through all the battle, Christ is winning because He has already won!

There had been, of course, intense battle and conflict from the birth of the Lord Jesus until Calvary. The enemy did everything in his power to frustrate the realization of the purpose of God in the Lord Jesus. He failed and Jesus won! His death on the cross spelt total victory over Satan and the powers of darkness, and by it He has brought them to nought. By His cross, He has despoiled, or disarmed, the principalities and the powers, making a show of them openly, triumphing over them in it (see Hebrews 2:14; Colossians 2:14–15, cf. NASB, "having stripped the principalities and the authorities" YLT).

The truth that the Apocalypse underlines is simple: *the Messiah rules in the midst of His enemies*! The enthronement of Christ has not ended satanically inspired conflict and battle; indeed, it will continue and intensify until He returns. His present enthronement guarantees the final fulfillment of God's Eternal Purpose, and the end of Satan and the powers of evil and darkness.

The holy city, the New Jerusalem, will come down out of heaven from God, having the glory of God (see Revelation 21:10–11).

He has won the battle for the completion of His work in us

The tremendous and encouraging truth in this last book of the Bible is simple but profound: the Lord Jesus has won the battle! He has not only won the battle for our salvation, but for the completion of His work in us. No matter how great the obstacles we face, or the difficult circumstances in which we find ourselves, or the many tribulations which beset us in the path laid out before us, He has won the battle for us. His enthronement means that everything you and I need to reach "the prize of the high calling of God in Christ Jesus" has been obtained (see Philippians 3:14). We have only to possess what He has won for us. As Paul said to Timothy: "Fight the good fight of faith; take hold of the eternal life to which you were called . . . " (1 Timothy 6:12 NASB). His finished work at Calvary spells total victory, and in His resurrection life is all the power we need. The key is *taking hold* of that life!

He has won the battle for the building of His Church

His enthronement also means that He has won the battle for the building of His Church. Everything needed for the completion of that work, He has won. The gates of death and hell may, at times, assault that building work. Indeed, at times it may seem as if Satan and the powers of darkness are winning, and the building work is paralyzed, if not overrun. Nevertheless, it is the Father Himself who has said to the Messiah: "Sit thou at my right hand, until I make thine enemies thy footstool" (Psalm 110:1). True church history furnishes us with all the evidence we need! Repeatedly the Holy Spirit has initiated powerful movements that have set forward the building work of the Lord Jesus. In the last era of world history, the Word of God predicts that the enemy will seem to obtain the upper hand. It will make no difference whatsoever to the enthronement of the Lord Jesus, for He has won! The building work of the Church will be completed and the marriage supper of the Lamb will take place.

He has won the battle for the work of God on the earth

The Lord Jesus has also won the battle for the work of God on this earth. What enormous conflict and battles beset the true servants of the Lord! What pressure and stress those suffer who are totally faithful to Him and to His purpose. Nevertheless for the work God commands, He always provides. All the grace and all the power needed to fulfill one's service or ministry have already been won by the Lord Jesus *at Calvary*. On *that* basis, the clothing, the gifts, and the equipment to fulfill His work are all made a reality through the outpoured Holy Spirit. Before His servants, the Lord opens doors that no one can shut and shuts doors that no one can open! He furnishes them with the keys of the kingdom to fulfill His will, no matter how great the problems, or how mountainous the difficulties which confront them (see Matthew 16:19). As long as a servant of God is doing the will of God, all the provision he or she requires is made available.

He that doeth the will of God abideth forever – C.T. Studd

God used the testimony of C.T. Studd to bring me to salvation. Indeed, his biography written by Norman Grubb was the first Christian book I ever read. C.T. Studd served the Lord with an utter and radical devotion not often found in the work of the

Lord. He served first in China, then in India, and finally in the Congo, Africa. Once he left Great Britain, he never returned until he went to be with the Lord. He was a pioneer and, like many pioneers, was not an easy man with whom to work. Norman Grubb, his son-in-law, told me that as he lay dying in the Congo, he said: "No matter what I should have been, or I should not have been, one thing I can say: whatever He told me to do, I have done." It was absolutely true and is the explanation for the growth of one of the most remarkable missionary fellowships and works in the history of the work of God on this earth. He was the exemplification of the words, "he that doeth the will of God abideth for ever" (1 John 2:17). For C.T. Studd, God opened a door, and no one has been able to close it. He and the work he began are an illustration of the simple truth: what God commands, for that He provides.

Chapter 9

THE GOLDEN LAMPSTAND AND THE TESTIMONY OF JESUS

We now face a surprising fact. We would expect that the enthroned Lamb would be the first vision which John beheld and recorded, for out of it everything else in the book unfolds. Instead, however, of occupying the first chapters, that vision is found in the *fourth* and *fifth* chapters. This fact in no way devalues its importance, for it is foundational to everything which the Holy Spirit is communicating in the Apocalypse.

The first vision, however, that John actually beheld and recorded, was of the risen Christ in the midst of seven golden lampstands (see Revelation 1:12–20). This was not by chance, nor is it a coincidence, for it is plain that the Holy Spirit had a design in this order. There is in fact a significant correspondence between the first three chapters of this book and the last two chapters. In understanding this connection, we will gain an understanding of the work the Holy Spirit has to do in us to bring us to God's goal. Within the full and complete salvation of God, all the grace and the power to reach His objective has been provided. We can add nothing to the finished work of Christ, but it is essential that we practically avail ourselves of the provision He has made within it. I have repeatedly emphasized this practical and vital truth: *we have to lay hold on that freely provided grace and power.*

Recognizing the connection between the beginning and the end of Revelation

In the first three chapters of Revelation, we discover seven golden lampstands: "I saw seven golden lampstands" (1:12 mg). See charts v and vi. In the last two chapters, we hear the words:

> the city . . . hath no need of the sun, neither of the moon, to shine upon it: for the glory of God did lighten it, and the lamp thereof is the Lamb. And the nations shall walk amidst the light thereof . . .
>
> (Revelation 21:23–24)

Note that the glory of God is the light, the lamp is the Lamb, and apparently the city is the lampstand. "The lamp thereof is the Lamb" is a most unusual phrase, and it leads us to the conviction that the symbolism is related to the lampstand all of gold. In the first three chapters, we have the risen and glorified Messiah walking "in the midst of the seven golden lampstands" (2:1). He is commending, correcting, judging, and encouraging the saints. In the last two chapters, we hear the words: "Behold, the tabernacle of God is with men, and he shall dwell with them . . . " And again: "I saw no temple therein: for the Lord God the Almighty, and the Lamb, are the temple thereof" (21:3, 22). In the first chapters, He is walking in the midst, with a work to do; in the last chapters, He is at home in His eternal dwelling place. In the first three chapters, we discover that these lampstands are made out of pure gold. We also hear the Lord saying to one of the churches, "I counsel thee to buy of me gold refined by fire" (3:18). In the last chapters, we discover that the whole city is produced out of pure gold, as transparent as glass.

In the first three chapters, we are told that the seven lampstands are seven churches on earth, in time, and in place. In the last three chapters, the work of the Holy Spirit in the churches is completed: we have the city of God, the New Jerusalem; the bride, the wife of the Lamb.

In the first three chapters, in every message which the Lord Jesus, the Head of the Church, gives to the churches, He speaks of overcoming (see Revelation 2:7, 11, 17, 26; 3:5, 12, 21). The Lord places a serious and real emphasis on an essential and vitally important matter. In the last chapters we hear the words:

> He that overcometh shall inherit these things; and I will be his God, and he shall by my son.
>
> (Revelation 21:7)

There is a real connection between overcoming in those churches on earth and in time, and inheriting the city of God, the wife of the Lamb. We should also note that in every one of the messages which He gives concerning overcoming, He also speaks of the necessity of spiritual hearing: "He that hath an ear, let him hear what the Spirit saith to the churches." Spiritual hearing is linked to overcoming, and is an essential factor in it.

The Risen Messiah in the midst of seven golden lampstands

It is a magnificent vision with which the Revelation of John opens. It begins with the Lord Jesus, the Messiah, in the midst of these lampstands. Clearly, it is meant to introduce us to the whole of the book. Are these the same golden lampstands which were found in the tabernacle and in the temple, and in the vision which Zechariah had? (See Exodus 25:31; 1 Kings 7:49; Zechariah 4:1–14.) It is obvious that the lampstand of the tabernacle and of the temple is the same lampstand which Zechariah also saw. In Hebrew, it is *menorah:* it can be a lampstand with one lamp, two or more lamps, or seven lamps. In those instances, it is the seven-branched menorah.

Is this seven-branched lampstand the same lampstand as those lampstands in Revelation? The Greek word translated by the English word "candlestick" or "lampstand" is *luchnia*. In the world of the Bible, it was more common to have oil lamps than wax candles, since there was an abundant supply of olive oil. The mention of a lampstand with a single lamp in Matthew 5:15–16 has led many to believe that the lampstands in the first three chapters of Revelation are the same kind of lampstand. For many serious Bible students, this idea is reinforced by the fact that the Lord Jesus was speaking about the testimony His children should bear.

In my estimation, however, it would be strange if a symbol as important as the seven-branched lampstand used throughout the Old Testament is changed to a lampstand with a single lamp in the concluding book of the Bible, especially since in both the Old Testament and the New Testament the lesson is the same: it is a question of divine light, of witness and of testimony.

The vision that Zechariah had of the golden lampstand greatly helps us to understand its significance. For Zechariah, it was clearly related to the rebuilding of the house of God. It is also noteworthy that the two branches of the olive trees on either side of the lampstand represent, on the one hand, Zerubbabel, the governor (who was of the royal seed), and, on the other hand, Joshua, the high priest (see Haggai 1:2; Ezra 5:1, 2). They were the two branches of the two olive trees. The two olive trees represent the two vital ministries: the kingship or the kingdom and the priesthood. Interestingly, they are emptying out of themselves gold which in turn becomes fuel for the lamps of the lampstand (see Zechariah 4:12 mg, cf. JND). The Hebrew of this verse is quite clear: it is not golden oil! It is gold that is being emptied out of redeemed men. Thus we have the same picture of ministry and service as in the Apocalypse, kingship and priesthood; the same object, the House of the Lord; the same theme of a vitally necessary building program; and the same need of *gold* to be produced in us: fuel for the light.

We are told that these seven lampstands represent seven churches. The figure seven in the Word of God symbolizes fullness, or completeness. The Lord chose these seven churches to represent the whole Church of God on earth, in time, and in place. There was no other division recognized in the early Church than that of geography. All those born of God in any given place were the church in that place. Whether we interpret these seven churches as the Church of God through history, or whether we see them as merely representing the whole Church of God on earth, at any time, and in named places, the lesson is the same. It is the sphere of the building work of Christ through the Holy Spirit. It is where Christ is building *His* Church, and that work is eternal. The Word of God states this truth simply: "in whom the whole building, being fitted together is growing into a holy temple in the Lord, in whom you also are being built together into a dwelling of God in the Spirit" (Ephesians 2:21–22 NASB). Note carefully *"in whom* the whole building . . . *in whom* you also are being built together into a dwelling of God in the Spirit." In whom? In Christ!

To be part of the church is to be *in Christ*. In Christ I discover all my brothers and sisters, those who like me have been born of the Spirit of God. We belong to each other. The apostle Paul, by the Spirit of God, stated it plainly:

> God is faithful, through whom ye were called into the fellowship of his Son Jesus Christ our Lord.
>
> (1 Corinthians 1:9)

He explained this even more clearly when he wrote:

> For even as we have many members in one body, and all the members have not the same office: so we, who are many, are one body in Christ, and severally members one of another.
>
> (Romans 12:4–5)

Note that it is "the fellowship of his Son," and it is "one body in Christ." It is not fellowship with His Son, vitally important as that is; it is the fellowship *of* His Son! It is not "one body of Christ"; it is "one body *in* Christ." We who are saved by the grace of God are *in this fellowship*; we are *one body in Christ*, and severally members one of another. Only the Holy Spirit can reveal the true nature of the church to a believer, but that illumination is essential.

If we are in Christ, we are part of the church. The idea that the church is a sacred physical building, or a certain denomination, is foreign to the New Testament. If you are in Christ, you are in the church. If you are not in Christ, no amount of rites or ceremonies will make you a part of His church. Charles Haddon Spurgeon once said: "You can be baptized all the way from Lands End [the western tip of the British Isles] to New England [in the United States], and all that will happen is that you will get very wet."

If your concept of the church is of an ecclesiastical or religious building, where you can lose your Bible, or leave your umbrella, or where you sit in pews or chairs, you will be totally lost over what I have written. Even if your concept of the church is of an ancient institution or a well-oiled organization or a hierarchical system, you will still be as lost. In this matter, we need to be granted a spirit of wisdom and revelation in the knowledge of Christ (see Ephesians 1:17).

If we are in Christ, we are the true church, whether at home or at work or at play. We cannot "*un-church*" ourselves! We are not the church only when we meet together; that is the *gathered* church (see Acts 14:27; cf. Hebrews 10:25). Once we have been born of God, we are in Christ and therefore always the church.

The meaning of the church is that we are in Christ and Christ is in us. We also see this vital truth in the words of the Lord Jesus:

> I am the true vine, and my Father is the husbandman . . . I am
> the vine, ye are the branches: He that abideth in me, and I in
> him, the same beareth much fruit: for apart from me ye can
> do nothing.
>
> (John 15:1, 5)

The vine was always a picture or an illustration of the covenant people of God. This declaration of the Lord Jesus must
have been for the disciples one of the most difficult to understand. If He had said, "I am the owner of the vine," or, "I am
the producer of the wine," it would have been understandable.
How could He say, "I am the people of God"! Nevertheless, He
explains it. We are to abide in Him, and He in us. By a new and
spiritual birth, God has positioned us in Christ, and Christ in us.
This is the church! Apart from Christ, there is no church. If *He*
is not building the church, it is not *His* church. It is nothing; it is
meaningless! Apart from Christ we can do nothing.

The testimony of Jesus

The churches are meant to hold the testimony of Jesus, in the
same manner in which the lampstand holds the lamps. This striking phrase "the testimony of Jesus" is found principally in this
last book of the Bible (see Revelation 1:2, 9; 12:17; 19:10; 20:4;
cf. 1 Corinthians 1:6). It is of tremendous significance. What is
the testimony of Jesus? It is interesting to note the way in which
John speaks of himself as being "in the isle that is called Patmos,
for the word of God and the testimony of Jesus" (Revelation
1:9). The testimony of Jesus is essentially linked with the Word
of God.

Jesus is the Word of God. When John wrote his gospel, he
wrote:

> In the beginning was the Word, and the Word was with God,
> and the Word was God . . . And the Word became flesh, and

dwelt among us (and we beheld his glory, glory as of the only
begotten from the Father), full of grace and truth.

(John 1:1, 14)

The Greek word *logos*, translated into English by "word," means
an unexpressed thought expressed in word; the unknown mind
articulated. In speech, a thought of the mind is articulated or is
uttered, otherwise the thought is unintelligible to others. The
Lord Jesus is the mind and the heart of God revealed. He is the
language of God. He is the invisible and living God, Who dwells
"in light unapproachable; whom no man hath seen, nor can
see . . .," revealed, expressed, and articulated. The Messiah said
of Himself, "I am the Alpha and the Omega," the A and the Z,
and everything in between. I am the Alphabet of God. In Him
we hear God; in Him we see God; in Him we touch God; and
in Him we become one with God! This is the testimony of Jesus
that the church is to hold.

A living and true church is meant to hold the testimony of
Jesus. It is designed to be a light bearer, and the Lord Jesus is the
only light it has. It is meant to be a witness and a testimony to
the whole world, shining in the darkness with a divine light that
cannot be overcome. To hold the testimony of Jesus is therefore
to be Christ-centered. He will be the center and circumference
of everything; all the avenues will lead to Him. Such a church
will abide in the quality of first love, continually being realigned
to Him by the Holy Spirit.

The essential link between the Word of God and the testimony of Jesus

We need to note the link between the Word of God and the testimony of Jesus. There is no way in which a church can hold the
testimony of Jesus and devalue the Word of God. Backsliding
and apostasy in church history have always begun with the
dethronement of the Lord Jesus and the devaluation of the Word

of God. Where there is a church that holds fast to the testimony of Jesus, you will always find in it an utter devotion to the Lord Jesus, and a readiness to obey the Word of God, whatever the cost. In a day when humanism and relativism have invaded the Church of God, and like a cancer have spread to every part of church life, it is of the utmost importance to give heed to this matter. We need to give to the Lord Jesus the supremacy and pre-eminence, the place that the Father has given Him. We need also to recognize the absolute authority of the Word of God *in all its parts*. Concerning these two issues there can be no compromise. They are both directly related to holding the testimony of Jesus.

The removal of the lampstand

The church is nothing when it has lost the testimony of Jesus. Speaking to the church at Ephesus, the Lord warned them that if they did not repent and return to their first love, He would remove their lampstand. With both the church at Ephesus and at Laodicea, it is interesting to consider what would have happened if the lampstand had been removed. Would anyone, including the elders, have noticed? The meetings would have rumbled on: the Bible study, the prayer meeting, the breaking of bread, and possibly even the evangelistic outreach. Would anything have changed? The first meeting, or gathering, to die slowly would have been the prayer meeting, and the second would have been the Bible study. The Lord's table would have become an "in memoriam" service, and evangelistic outreach would have seemed to be too unsophisticated, and even offensive. If we accept the evidence of church history, everything would have slowly degenerated into a crystallized system, into an ecclesiastical routine, without the powerful resurrection life of Christ and the fire of the Holy Spirit. There is no possibility of reaching the fulfillment of God's Eternal Purpose when the testimony of Jesus is no longer held, and the Word of God is no longer obeyed.

The testimony of Jesus is the spirit of prophecy

When John sought to worship the angel who was revealing these matters to him, the angel said: "I am a fellow servant with thee and with thy brethren that hold the testimony of Jesus: worship God; for the testimony of Jesus is the spirit of prophecy" (Revelation 19:10). This reveals that the testimony of Jesus is, by its nature, prophetic. When I write this, I am not writing about only predictive prophecy or even the gift of prophetic utterance, but about the essential meaning of prophecy: the forth-telling of the heart and the mind of God. In other words, when the testimony of Jesus is held by a church, there is in that assembly a prophetic content: there is a manifestation of the heart and mind of God in and through the Lord Jesus. This is also true of all who are members of the body of Christ, the church, and all those who seek to serve Him and His purpose. Their lives, their service, and even their circumstances have the same prophetic content.

Thus from this statement made by the angel to John, it seems clear that the holding of the testimony of Jesus is prophetic. When a church or an assembly holds the testimony of Jesus, its ministry, its service, and its life, its very existence, become prophetic! It is the heart and mind of God expressed and revealed in and through saved human beings. If an unsaved man or woman comes into such a gathering of believers, he or she instantly senses that God is there. In such an atmosphere, the most godless and depraved can be touched, impacted, and saved, and miracles of healing, of deliverance, and of salvation take place.

When God is at home

Every human being seeks a home! When God is "at home" in a church, the unsaved witness to it, even if they cannot explain their inner feeling. This is partly what was meant by the apostle Paul when he wrote: "the secrets of his heart are made manifest;

and so he will fall down on his face and worship God, declaring that God is among you indeed" (1 Corinthians 14:25). In the previous verses, he speaks of the gift of tongues and of prophetic utterance, manifesting the presence of the Lord. Essentially it means that the presence of God in such a community of believers will touch the unbeliever in their midst. When Jesus was on this earth, everywhere He went He touched the unsaved, the society dropouts and the outcasts, the hopeless and the needy, and brought them to God. Those unsaved ones touched the heart of God in Him, and were in turn touched by the love of God through Him, and were never the same again. This is the testimony of Jesus.

Would to God that every community of believers called a church was like that! An expression of God's home! So often such communities can have all the sound doctrine, all the normal routine of church life, but the most essential factor is missing. When the testimony of Jesus is held by a church, the heart of God is present.

Chapter 10

WHAT IS THE CHURCH?

The Church was born on the Jewish festival of Shavuot. Shavuot, which simply means "weeks," was seven weeks or forty-nine days, counted from the second day of Passover. The festival of Shavuot was held on the fiftieth day, hence the Greek "Pentecost," or "fiftieth." It was one of the three obligatory pilgrimage festivals of the year: Passover, or Pesach; Pentecost, or Shavuot; and the Feast of Tabernacles, or Sukkot. Every Jewish man above the age of twelve was obliged to "appear before the Lord in the temple" on these three festivals. We are told it was on the Day of Pentecost, "when it was fully come," that the Holy Spirit was poured out upon a small company of faithful believers who had been gathering together steadfastly for some ten days.

On that day, one hundred and twenty individual units of a "perfect" congregation were transformed into one hundred and twenty members of the body of Christ. It was revolutionary. Never before in the long history of the Old Testament had anything like this taken place. It was the pouring out of the long-promised Holy Spirit by the risen, glorified Messiah, Jesus, on the basis of His finished work (see e.g. Ezekiel 36:26–27; Joel 2:28–29; cf. Jeremiah 31:31–34). On many occasions the Holy Spirit had fallen on individuals, empowering and using them, and enabling them to prophesy or to work miracles. Now the

Holy Spirit came to *indwell* saved men and women. He did not come to visit them, or to use them, but to make His abode, His permanent dwelling place, in them.

The one hundred and twenty disciples in the upper room were disciples indeed! This handful of believers was the fruit of the Messiah's ministry. We may well ask what had happened to the thousands fed by the Lord on at least two occasions; or the thousands who had heard the Sermon on the Mount, or who had heard the messages He gave in the temple, or elsewhere in Jerusalem; or the many that had come for healing or deliverance? In the end, it was these faithful followers of the Lord Jesus, a truly small company of disciples, who now remained together for some ten days, waiting on the Lord, in fervent prayer and supplication, for the fulfillment of His promise concerning the Holy Spirit.

A perfect church?

In many ways they represent a perfect "church": they had all the features that we generally associate with a good church! They were gathered in the name of Christ alone; they were meeting with one accord; they were united in their worship and love for Christ; they had no doubt about the authority and inspiration of the Word of God (at that point of time only the Old Testament); since Jesus had opened their understanding of the Scriptures, they would have been searching them and studying them every day. They were also absolutely clear on the person and work of the Lord Jesus: His virgin birth; His sinlessness; the three years of His Messianic ministry, confirmed by many signs and miracles; His atoning death; His bodily resurrection and His ascension which they had witnessed. They also believed in His literal return in power and great glory. They believed in the power of prayer, and gave themselves to it with devotion and persistence.

For many Christians, this would be a perfect church, the kind of church it is believed that would come as a result of revival; the type of church that many Christians would like to join. Indeed, many of us would be more than satisfied if the fellowship we attend was of this caliber. Why then, we may well ask, did the Lord adamantly command them to remain in Jerusalem until the promise of the Father came upon them and they would be clothed with power from on high? (See Luke 24:49; Acts 1:4–5.) It seems as if the Lord Jesus was concerned that, let loose, they would raise up such congregations wherever they could! They would have built up assemblies with the same form and structure, in principle, as the temple and the synagogue in the Old Testament period. The emphasis would have been on special "sanctified" buildings and places, on distinct orders of people dressed in special clothes, on an organization separate from the Head, rather than an organic union with the Head. The outpouring of the Holy Spirit marked an essential change from the outward to the inward, from the natural to the spiritual. From this point in time, the work of the Lord was in another dimension.

The objective of the Holy Spirit's indwelling and empowering

What was the real and essential work that the Holy Spirit performed on that Day of Pentecost? Was it only that they were given new power and life, and that they spoke in tongues and prophesied? I have no doubt about the necessity of the power and the life of the Holy Spirit. His person and His work are obviously foundational to everything. Moreover, it is His unique work to substantiate and make real the powerful resurrection life of the Messiah. Similarly, I have also no doubt concerning the necessity of the gifts and the equipment of the Holy Spirit. They are essential for the work of the Lord. What, however, was *the objective and aim* of His empowering and indwelling, and of the gifts and equipment which He brought with Him? It is of real importance to recognize that the gale force wind, the fire which parted and was distributed into one hundred and twenty flames, the power which was manifested in that upper room, the tongues and the prophesying were all the evidence of something even more basic and foundational.

The Head in heaven by the Holy Spirit joined to the body on earth

On that day when the Holy Spirit came, the Head, at the right hand of God the Father, was joined to the body on earth. For the first time in history, one hundred and twenty saved sinners had been joined to a risen, glorified Messiah by the indwelling power of the Holy Spirit. Some seven weeks earlier, Jesus had won our salvation, and the great veil in the temple had been torn in two, from top to bottom. That veil had separated God from man, but now it had been torn in two, signifying that God and man, in the Messiah, were reconciled. It was a momentous act of God, and the outpouring of the Holy Spirit now made that reconciliation and salvation a living practical reality. It was a spiritual explosion! He made that small group of weak, frail human beings members of the body of the Messiah. The English word "members" is the Greek word *melos*, meaning "limbs" or "members." It does not denote members of a society, or an organization, or a club, but body members, parts or limbs of a body.

It is clear that God's objective and aim in the outpouring of the Holy Spirit was to produce a living union of the Head and the members of the body. Indeed, the Word of God states:

> For as the body is one, and hath many members, and all the members of the body, being many, are one body; so also is Christ.
>
> (1 Corinthians 12:12)

A powerful, invincible spiritual *organism* had been brought to birth by the coming of the Holy Spirit. That spiritual union of head and body was something the world had never before witnessed. Normal human beings, saved by the grace of God, were now, by the person of the Holy Spirit, introduced to another dimension, a spiritual and an eternal dimension. Everything that happened on that day was evidence that those saved men and women had become the recipients of the resurrection life and power of the Lord Jesus: they were joined to Him in the unity of the Spirit. They were not only born of the Spirit, but by the Spirit they were experiencing His risen life. Within that life, they would discover all the grace and the power of God, which He had made available to them. All the fruit which the Holy Spirit produces, and all the gifts which He manifests, were in that life of Christ.

This "era changing event" was manifested in dynamic power: hurricane force wind, like a typhoon, filled the building; divine fire appeared, and was divided to dwell on each one of those present; for the first time in their lives, they spoke in tongues; those who had only read the prophets, and listened to the Lord Jesus prophesy, themselves now prophesied! To many onlookers they seemed to be inebriated, drunk with wine. Within an hour or two, 3000 Jews had been born of God and were also immediately joined to the Head at the right hand of God, as the one hundred and twenty disciples had been earlier joined to Him. They had all become one body in Christ.

It was the presence of God that was manifested in great glory and power on that day. The temple in Jerusalem, the house of the Lord, was the place where, figuratively, the presence of God was to be found. There He met with His own covenanted and redeemed people: even then He met with only one person, the high priest, and that only once a year when the high priest entered the holy of holies. On each of the occasions when the tabernacle and the temple had been completed, the glory of God had filled the whole place (see Exodus 40:34–35; 2 Chronicles 7:1–3). Now the presence of God, by the Holy Spirit, filled 3120 saved men and women. God had come home! The impact on Jerusalem was to be colossal.

In the same manner in which a human body is the expression of its head, the church is to be the expression of the Lord Jesus, its Head. Through His body, He expresses His love, His grace, His compassion, and His mercy; and also His righteousness, His holiness, and His justice. He also expresses His will and His mind through that body. It is to be the manifestation of the presence of God on earth. Through the church, the presence of God touches the sinner, however lost or depraved he or she may be; and the world in all its loneliness, its hopelessness, and its homelessness touches God. The world is meant to find God "at home" in the church. This is the meaning of holding the testimony of Jesus.

The key: the enthroned Christ as Head of the body

The key to this fulfillment of God's promise to pour out the Holy Spirit is found first and foremost in the enthronement of the Lord Jesus. On His ascension, He was enthroned but not yet crowned. His coronation is yet to be! He was enthroned as King of kings and Lord of lords, as ruler of the kings of the earth, as the King of Israel; *and as the Head of the Church*, which is His body. This concept of "head and body" is only found in the New Testament (see Colossians 1:18; 2:19; Ephesians 1:22–23; 4:15–16; 5:23).

The term "head and body" in the New Testament is often misunderstood. We think of the Head of the body, Christ, as if He is the head of a college, the chancellor of a university, the prime minister in a cabinet, or the principal of a hospital. The Word of God uses it in its proper sense: the head and the body are one living organism! A headless body is dead; a bodiless head is just as dead. The New Testament picture requires an organic union between head and body. That is the church.

The difference between an organism and an organization

The difference between an organization and an organism is the difference between something static and something living. An organism has a considerable and remarkably intricate organization, but the origin and source of that organization is totally within its life. The "organization" of an organization cannot change unless it is altered from an external source. Otherwise, it will always remain the same. A car that is a 1980 model remains a 1980 model unless it is updated, and it can only be updated and modernized from without. On the other hand, my body is a 1931 model and, throughout my life, has been continuously renewed from within, so that I am reasonably contemporary! Everything that I am today came from 1931, but my body has grown and matured and is still today a contemporary body. This is the difference between an organization and an organism! The church is an organism, not an organization. It should always be in a state of renewal, and therefore contemporary.

On the one hand, we are to "contend earnestly for the faith which was *once for all delivered unto the saints*" (Jude 1:3, author's emphasis). We have been given no mandate or authority to revise it, or to revamp it, in order to make it more acceptable to the modern outlook. When we reinterpret the Word of God to suit contemporary society, it is no longer God's Word, but the word of man. The gospel we preach then becomes another gospel! On the other hand, the church as the body of Christ should be constantly renewed, alive, and up to date. That should be its normal condition.

Whilst in union with the Head the body is invincible

The headship of Christ in the church is *the* essential factor. The enemy's strategy has not changed from the early days of the Church until today. It is to divorce the body from the Head.

Anything or anyone that comes between the head and the body of Christ brings paralysis, lifelessness, and death. It is the story of the church on earth! Leadership of any kind, whether elderships, pastorates, councils, committees, or boards, can either hear the Lord and obey Him, with life-giving results, or substitute what they consider to be the will of the Lord for what is actually His will, with disastrous consequences. So often talk and voting takes the place of seeking the Lord. The real key is seeking the Lord for His mind and His will in any given matter, and giving time to wait together upon Him until we discern His will.

The Lord Jesus stated this truth in utter simplicity:

> My sheep hear my voice, and I know them, and they follow me.
>
> (John 10:27)

And again, as we have already noted, the Lord Jesus underlined this matter of hearing Him when He said to each of the seven churches: "He that hath an ear, let him hear what the Spirit saith to the churches." The history of the Church proves that when the leadership of the church, those responsible for the well-being of the flock, fail to hear His voice, the degeneration has begun. That always leads, in the end, to the removal of the lampstand. The outpouring of the Holy Spirit creates within the believer a hearing ear: it is a spiritual ability to hear what the Lord is saying. If one cannot hear the Master's voice and obey Him, one's service is meaningless.

Whilst by the Spirit of God the body of Christ *on earth* remained in living union with its Head *in heaven*, it was invincible. The whole of Jerusalem was turned upside down; neither the occupying Roman administration nor the Jewish establishment were able to halt its progress. It spread throughout Judea and Samaria. In Samaria the enormous alienation between the Jews and the Samaritans was overcome in those who were born of God: they fellowshipped together as one body in Christ. Finally it reached Caesarea, a basically Gentile city, and the headquarters of the Roman administration in the land of Israel. When the Holy Spirit fell on those Gentile officers and their families, and the other Gentiles who were present, as He had fallen upon the Jews and also upon the Samaritans, it was an incredible point that had been reached in divine history. For the first time, full-blooded Gentiles were born of the Spirit of God and joined to the Head, the Lord Jesus, at God's right hand, and to their Jewish brothers and sisters! The middle wall of partition had been abolished in the Messiah. They became equals, fellow heirs, fellow members of the same body, and fellow partakers of the same promise in the Messiah (see Ephesians 2:14; 3:6).

All this happened without any of the usual paraphernalia we associate with Christian work and evangelism. There was no huge campaign of advertisement, other than by word of mouth; there were no boards or committees; no fundraising schemes; there was no need for the training of campaign personnel. There were only men and women, saved by the grace of God, filled with the Holy Spirit, joined to their Head in heaven, and ready to obey Him. Although they overturned the known world, this would not meet modern requirements for evangelistic "outreach"; it would be considered impractical and far too mystical.

The progress of this work, which began at Pentecost, proved to be invincible whilst it remained in living union with the Head, in practical obedience to Him, and in the unity of the Spirit. Within a few decades, the gospel had covered all of the land of Israel and most of the Roman Empire, and beyond. It had reached Spain, France, and the British Isles, in the West; Egypt, the Sudan, and Ethiopia, in the South; Armenia in the North; and Persia and Iraq and even to the tip of southern India, in the East.

I will build My Church

The Lord Jesus made a declaration that was both dogmatic and explicit when He said: "upon this rock I will build my church; and the gates of Hades shall not prevail against it" (Matthew 16:18). The fact that there is on this earth a living and true Church is the evidence that Jesus is still building His Church. His building work has proved to be invincible. We see it today, principally, in the third world areas, in Asia, in China, in Africa, and in South America. Sadly, it is in the Western world, in the so-called "homelands" of the Church and the gospel, that His building work is threatened by lukewarmness, backsliding, superficiality, compromise, apostasy, and plain heresy. None of this is surprising, although sad and painful to those who care for the testimony of Jesus on this earth.

The gates of hell and death have sought to prevail against the building work of the Lord Jesus throughout these two millennia. Very often, Satan's tactics have been to use those in the church to plant a "Trojan horse" within it, and thus paralyze and destroy it. Affluent lukewarmness has led to serious compromise with the world, and the contradiction of everything it was meant to be. The so-called church has then become a worldly force and power, as dark as the world in which it was supposed to be a light. It became a proud and self-sufficient institution, a persecutor and a murderer of those who were faithful to the Lord. The evidence for this is in church history. It is also in the record that has been and is still being compiled, at the right hand of God.

Those gates of hell and death have never finally prevailed against the building work of the Lord Jesus. The literal rendering of the Greek is "the gates of Hades." "Hades" is the Greek name for the place of departed spirits. It means little to most believers. I prefer to use the KJV translation, "the gates of hell." It is not as literally correct as "gates of Hades," but conveys the spiritual idea in a much better and more meaningful way. The concept expressed in this phrase is of satanic and demonic force and power, using spiritual death as its weapon. Gates in the Bible symbolize government policy, the administration of justice, and intercourse. The gates of hell symbolize the strategy and policies of Satan and his hierarchy. These gates represent the powers of spiritual death, darkness and evil, which have assaulted the building work of the Lord Jesus repeatedly, and have sometimes seemed to have prevailed and won. In fact, they have neither prevailed nor won. The Holy Spirit has again and again initiated new movements that have returned the redeemed people of God to the original course. In those movements, truths that were first compromised and then lost have been gloriously recovered and restored; for example, to name a few of those truths: the absolute Authority, Inspiration, and practical Relevance of the Bible; Justification by Faith Alone; the Priesthood of all Believers; and the Necessity of the New Birth.

The Head in action through the body

When Luke wrote the book of the Acts, he began with the words:

> The former treatise I made, O Theophilus, concerning all that Jesus began both to do and to teach, until the day in which he was received up . . .
>
> (Acts 1:1–2)

We should note carefully the words "began both to do and to teach." Luke, with his normal concern for precision, clearly considered the book of the Acts to be the continuation of what Jesus began to do and to teach. In other words, he saw the whole story of the Acts as the illustration and evidence of that continuation! Only now, the Lord Jesus was directing everything from God's right hand. It was the Head in action through the body. Luke understood that through the finished work of the

Lord Jesus, and the pouring out by Him of the Holy Spirit, a living, powerful, and invincible "organism" had been born at Pentecost. It was Head and body joined together in one living union. Whilst churches discerned, through the Holy Spirit, the will and the mind of the Head, and were obedient to Him, they proved to be invincible: nothing could stop their progress. It was a door opened by the Head in heaven, which no one on earth could close, nor even satanic principalities or powers.

It is an interesting fact that the book of Acts is seemingly open ended. It appears to have no conclusion. What is the significance of this fact? Did Luke just fade out, or was he depressed by the manner in which Paul met the end of his earthly life? I think not. The answer is simple. The account of the Acts of the Holy Spirit did not conclude with the twenty-eighth chapter, but has proceeded throughout the history of the Church until the present day. The record of the true Church is still being made by the Lord, and one day at the coming down of the New Jerusalem, the Wife of the Lamb, He will conclude the book of Acts!

Whenever the Holy Spirit has fallen upon saved men and women, practically joining them to the Head in heaven, we have the same manifestation of the presence of God on earth, the same experience of resurrection life and power, the same awareness and discernment of the mind of the Head, the same devotion and obedience to the Lord and His Word, and the same incredible and dynamic results. Whole nations and even empires have been turned upside down by such true and faithful disciples. Even worldly society and its practices have been reformed and changed. It matters not where we look in the long history of the Church that Christ is building: it is the same story. It is a rediscovery of the essential meaning of Calvary and of Pentecost, and that rediscovery in experience always turns the world upside down!

The building work of the Lord Jesus is invincible

The building work of the Lord Jesus has proved to be invincible. It will not cease until He has completed that work. The hatred of the world for those who belong to the Lord Jesus, the savage fury that they have vented on them, crucifying them, beheading them, feeding them to wild animals, drowning them, burning them at stakes, placing them in forced labor or concentration camps, has all proved to be in vain. Even when servants of God were imprisoned or martyred, it made no difference to that building work. Indeed, it only added glory to it, and further increase and multiplication. The last century has witnessed more martyrs than any other century since the birth of the Church, but, as always, the blood of the martyrs has proved to be the seed of the Church. It is true whether in Iran, or China, or Russia, or anywhere else! It is solid evidence of the invincibility of His work. The Lord Jesus, enthroned at the right hand of God, by the Holy Spirit has continued to build the real and true Church to this day, and will continue to build it until His coming in glory. Let us face the simple fact: Satan has lost and the Messiah has won!

Chapter 11

BEING BUILT TOGETHER AS THE HOME OF GOD

The Messiah declared that He Himself would build the Church, and proclaimed that the gates of hell would not prevail against it. It was to supervise that building work that the Holy Spirit came at Pentecost. As I have already pointed out, this building work has never ceased, in spite of the enormous attempts of the powers of darkness to paralyze it and destroy it. Furthermore, it is my understanding that if you and I are not part of it, we will not be able to reach the goal, the prize of the high calling of God in the Messiah Jesus. That reveals just how serious and practical this issue is.

Where, however, is this building work to be done? The answer to that question brings us to the heart of the matter. Most Christians would readily acknowledge that Christ is the builder, and that His building work is important. Is this work, however, fulfilled wholly in an unseen realm, so "spiritual" that there is no physical evidence for it? Many people relegate it to an unreal sphere, a realm in which it cannot be seen, felt, or tested. In actual fact it is true that all the accumulated value and worth of His building work goes into the heavenlies, into that realm which we can neither see nor touch; but the *practical work is done on earth*, in the ordinary and routine circumstances of everyday life.

The book of Revelation opens with the significant vision of the Head of the Church in the midst of seven churches. Those seven churches, representing the whole Church of God, in time and place, are directly related to the New Jerusalem and the bride of the Messiah. The gold, the precious stone, and the pearl, out of which the city of God and the bride are formed, have all to be produced in and through those churches. It is therefore in some way a comfort to discover how weak, how failing, and how very human they are! It is also a challenge to discover that we have to overcome in those churches.

We have been given this one, quickly passing, life in which all this work has to be done by the Holy Spirit. If we are in Christ, then we are in the Church somewhere on earth, and in time, whether we are aware of it or not. We are all found between the first three chapters of Genesis and the last three chapters of Revelation. In fact, we can narrow it down even more: in our day, we are to be found between the first three chapters and the last two chapters of the Apocalypse.

The churches are God's building yard

The churches then and now are a builder's yard, the yard of the Divine Builder. This practical work of building is centered in it. I asked the question, where is this building work to be done? The answer is clear: it is within those churches. That is the real meaning of the golden lampstands which represent them. Whilst the lampstand is in place, and the testimony of Jesus is still being held, the building process is on course. When the lampstand is removed, and the testimony of Jesus is withdrawn, the building process stops. The history of the Church furnishes us with abundant evidence of this. A church on earth, in time and in place, is meaningless unless there is a spiritual building work in progress!

Writing to believers, Paul said:

> So then you are no longer strangers and aliens, but you are
> fellow citizens with the saints, and are of God's household,
> having been built upon the foundation of the apostles and
> prophets, Christ Jesus Himself being the corner stone, in
> whom the whole building, being fitted together, is growing
> into a holy temple in the Lord; in whom you also are being
> built together into a dwelling of God in the Spirit.
>
> (Ephesians 2:19–22 NASB)

Note carefully that this is all about building: "having been
built"; "the whole building"; and "built together." We then
have vitally important related phrases: "corner stone"; "fitted
together"; "growing into a holy temple"; and "a dwelling of
God." From all of this, it becomes apparent that this building
work is essentially to do with the Lord Jesus. He is the corner
stone; in Him the whole building grows into a holy temple;
in Him you and I are being built together into a dwelling place
of God, a home of God in the Spirit. This truth is of paramount
importance to each one of us. Simply stated, it means that if
you and I are ignorant of this necessity, we are not going to
see any requirement to be built into a home of God in the
Spirit.

Unfortunately, it is not only ignorance of this truth but the
wrapping up of it in religiously archaic language that renders
it irrelevant to most ordinary Christians. We think of *growing
into a holy temple in the Lord* as something "in the air," as some
kind of Christian concept that has no practical application. It is
sad that the Greek word *oikodome* has been translated so often
by the English word "edify" or "edifying," instead of "build up"
or "building up." For most Christians, edification is associated
with mere biblical head knowledge; a kind of religious duty to
be performed between believers when meeting together, but
irrelevant to our daily living.

Let everything be done unto building up

The apostle Paul, however, did not understand it in that way. For him it was of profound practical importance. In all his letters, he speaks of the need for everything to be done for the "building up" of the church, or of individual believers. From the most important ministries, such as apostles, or prophets, or evangelists, or pastors, or teachers, to the most humble ministries, the aim of all was the building up of the body of Christ. Every true believer was to be fitly framed together in Christ, to grow into a holy temple in the Lord; to be built together into a home of God. On any account, such a building work would never be easy. To build together those who are saved by God, with their different temperaments, outlooks, and backgrounds, will generally prove difficult. The very process of fitting living stone to living stone is costly. The building work is essentially related to two matters: a holy temple in the Lord, and the home of God, the place of His dwelling. The temple represents living sacrifice, worship, prayer, intercession, and ministry. The dwelling of God, the home of God, represents love, fellowship, union and communion, and a shared life.

Built up a spiritual house

The apostle Peter writes of the same matter:

> unto whom coming, a living stone, rejected indeed of men, but with God elect, precious, ye also, as living stones are built up a spiritual house, to be a holy priesthood, to offer up spiritual sacrifices, acceptable to God through Jesus Christ.
>
> (1 Peter 2:4–5)

Peter also sees the essential necessity of God's children being built together. He writes of these living stones being built up as a spiritual house. A pile of stones is not a house, whether all over the place or neatly stacked. Those stones have to be fitted together. They have to find their relation to one another, in order to be built up as a spiritual house.

In the process of the renovation of my home in Jerusalem, I watched with fascination the old stonemasons building together the stones. The most elderly stonemason would take these rocks from a great heap and hold them up to his cheek, one by one, and then he either put certain ones on one side or threw others onto a pile. I suspected that he was going to take the pile of rocks away for his personal use, since they appeared to me to be exceedingly fine rocks! So I spoke to the chief contractor, who was a personal friend. He told me that this elderly stonemason was absolutely trustworthy, and that what he was doing was sorting out the faulty stones from those which were faultless. The stonemason did not want to spend time on fashioning a stone which, at the last moment, would split into two or shatter. The work on those stones was arduous and long, and I have never forgotten the sound of them being chipped and chiseled day after day, until finally they were ready. When that moment arrived, then began the long job of fitting the stones together until, finally, the work was completed.

It is not a quick or easy job to fashion saved human beings, but it is the work of the Holy Spirit. He chips and He chisels for as long as it is necessary, until He has the stones ready. The whole work is related to being "fitly framed together." In ancient times, no mortar was used: those stones had to be "fitted" together into one by a master mason or builder. Often he had to chip some material away from one stone in order to fit it to another. It is important to underline the phrases *"growing into* a holy temple in the Lord" and *"being built together into* a dwelling of God in the Spirit"*: they denote a process which takes time. Spiritually, for those whom God saves, who see the need to be built together, it is a costly business, but the end is exceedingly precious: a temple in the Lord; a dwelling or home of God in the Spirit.

These are the pictures or illustrations which the Holy Spirit uses in the building of God's spiritual house. In our case, both the work of shaping and chiseling and our being fitly framed together is a parallel process.

Being built together

What does it mean to be built together, or fitly framed together? It means that *together* we share His life: we have become "members [or limbs] one of another." We are still individuals, but we have lost our self-centered individualism. We can no longer live and act as if we are only individuals without any relation to anyone but God. The expression "members [or limbs] one of another" is an extraordinary phrase and worthy of consideration.

A Christian lady once said to me, "I and the Lord get on very well together; the problem is between me and other Christians." This illustrates the problem we face. It became apparent in the following years that she was deluded. Her so-called "life with the Lord" was a sham. It was a Christianized self-life, which could not bear the discipline of belonging to a spiritual family. When we are being built together as a spiritual house, we have that sense of belonging to one another, of being part of one another, of being "family." That can never be a fact unless we are committed to Christ in one another and prepared to open up to one another.

Indeed, it is true that if we are born of God, we belong to the whole family of God, whatever their color or race or tongue. We are one body in Christ: they belong to us, and we belong to them. However, it is only in the place where we live that the practical building together with other believers can be fulfilled. There the real work of building takes place. There also we discover that we cannot choose the stones to which we are being fitly framed: they are chosen for us by the Holy Spirit! This is a discipline, and only those committed to the building work of the

Lord will endure it. Nevertheless, it has serious consequences, for it is related to the possession of our inheritance.

A holy priesthood

It is important to underline that which, by the Holy Spirit, Peter wrote: "to be a holy priesthood, to offer up spiritual sacrifices acceptable to God through Jesus Christ." The priesthood of all believers is one of those truths that were recovered in the Reformation, even though in previous centuries there had been movements of the Spirit of God in which believers practiced it. Sadly, it was not many decades following the Reformation before that truth was contradicted, and a distinct division was made between "clergy" and "laity." The Word of God is very clear. All true believers born into the kingdom of God are made a kingship, and priests unto God (see e.g. Revelation 1:6; 5:10).

Every child of God, by virtue of their salvation, is constituted a priest to God, and has the right to offer up spiritual sacrifices to God acceptable through Jesus the Messiah. Not one of them requires another person to mediate between them and God. There is, of course, divine authority in the house of God, and it is vested by the Lord in certain brethren. We are commanded to obey those who as our leaders have the rule over us; to respect and to honor them (see Hebrews 13:17, cf. NASB, YLT). Nevertheless, under the Lord Jesus, the King, we are *all* a royal dominion, kings; and, under His High Priesthood, we are *all* priests unto God. This is the calling of *every* true child of God.

When the priesthood of all believers is contradicted, a serious paralysis develops in the body of Christ. The apostle Paul wrote:

> we are to grow up in all aspects into Him who is the head,
> even Christ, from whom the whole body, being fitted and held
> together by what every joint supplies, according to the proper

working of each individual part, causes the growth of the body
for the building up of itself in love.

(Ephesians 4:15–16 NASB)

Note very carefully: "according to the proper working of each
individual part." That is the priesthood of all believers in opera-
tion. When each individual member of the body of Christ is
functioning, there is no paralysis, but a growing up into Him
as head, and a growth of the body for the building up of itself
in love.

The priesthood of all believers is not just an antique doctrine,
to be revered as part of the Reformation, but basically contradicted in practice: it is *a practical and relevant necessity for spiritual
growth,* both personal and corporate. No church will ever function as it is meant to function in the mind of God without the
priesthood of all believers in action. Furthermore, this principle
is directly related to the golden lampstand and the holding of
the testimony of Jesus.

The lampstand all of gold represents a divine building program

The vision that the Lord gave to the prophet Zechariah, as it is
recorded in Zechariah 4, illustrates this essential truth. He saw
the seven-branched lampstand beaten out of pure gold. It was
the golden lampstand of both the tabernacle and the temple. He
also saw two olive trees, one on either side of the lampstand,
emptying gold out of two branches which became fuel for the
light of the lamps. Zechariah thought he was clear concerning
the significance of the golden lampstand, but was mystified over
the meaning of the two olive trees. Then it was revealed to him
that the lampstand and the two olive trees represented a divine
building program.

At that point, the house of the Lord was still badly ruined. The
work had begun on the foundation, and some renovation had

taken place, but had ceased. The halting of the work was due to enormous political and economic problems and obstacles. The prophet Haggai, by the Spirit of God, had put his finger on the problem. It was not that the Lord was powerless, but rather that the priorities of the people of God were not clear. They said: "The time has not come for the Lord's house to be built": that was the way they understood the economic and political problems which confronted the building work. The Lord said through Haggai: "Is it time for you yourselves to dwell in your paneled houses while this house lies desolate?" (see Haggai 1). The Lord revealed to them through the prophet Haggai that all their problems were due to wrong priorities. This has always been true. When the people of God make their own well-being a priority, and place no value on being built up and built together in the Lord, spiritual stagnation and paralysis follow.

We then become trapped in a cycle of life in a spiritual wilderness, as the children of Israel were trapped in an actual wilderness. It was a cycle that lasted thirty-eight years. The pillar of cloud and fire was there, and the manna, and the water out of the rock, and the many miracles of provision and protection, but the house of the Lord could only be built on the other side of the river Jordan, in the Promised Land, and only in Jerusalem. Their *inheritance* was in the Promised Land. It should have taken them two weeks, or at the most two years. Instead, it took forty years! Although they were out of Egypt, their hearts were in Egypt: Egypt was still *in* them. It was that link with the old life which caused the problem with priorities. The people of God learned this lesson painfully.

The question of priorities

When Zechariah and Haggai fulfilled their ministries, a remnant of the people of God was back in the Promised Land, and in Jerusalem. The foundation of the house of God had been laid, and the rebuilding work had commenced, but had ceased.

Mountainous obstacles and difficulties, spiritual, political, and economic, had confronted the builders, depressing and demoralizing them. Once again, the question of priorities had surfaced.

These seemingly complex and insoluble problems were no hindrance to God. The purpose of God would be fulfilled, and it would be realized through people who were redeemed and had a living relationship with the Lord. To Zechariah, the Lord revealed this:

> he [Zerubbabel] shall bring forth the top stone with shoutings of Grace, grace, unto it . . . The hands of Zerubbabel have laid the foundation of this house; his hands shall also finish it . . . For who hath despised the day of small things? For these seven shall rejoice, and shall see the plummet in the hand of Zerubbabel . . .
>
> (Zechariah 4:7, 9–10)

As I have repeatedly emphasized, the Lord made it clear that the lampstand represented a building program. All the phrases used by the Holy Spirit point to that: "the *top stone*"; "the hands of Zerubbabel *laid the foundation* of this house; his hands *shall also finish it*"; "the *plummet*" in his hand.

This building work could only be completed through the person and work of the Holy Spirit: "Not by might, nor by power, but by my Spirit, saith the Lord of hosts" (Zechariah 4:6). Those mountains confronting them would become a plain before Zerubbabel, as he went forward with the building work *in faith and obedience*.

It is interesting to note that in this vision you have the three vital ministries represented: Zerubbabel the governor, of the royal seed (see Matthew 1:12; Luke 3:27); Joshua the high priest (see Zechariah 3:1); and Zechariah and Haggai, the prophets. Zechariah had been preoccupied with the two olive trees, and with the two particular branches that were emptying the gold out of themselves into the lampstand. It was revealed to him that the branches were the governor and the high priest. The house of the Lord, however, would never have been rebuilt but for the prophetic ministry also of Zechariah and Haggai (see Ezra 5:1–2). In this connection, note the words: "the testimony of Jesus is the spirit of prophecy" (Revelation 19:10). For the rebuilding of the temple, it required the fulfillment of these three ministries: kingship, priesthood, and prophetic ministry.

Not by might, nor by power, but by My Spirit

All of this has tremendous import for us in the light of what we have said in this book. The summing up of everything in the last book of the Bible begins with the vision of the glorified Messiah in the midst of seven golden lampstands. As has already been pointed out, those lampstands represent seven churches. In fact, the lampstand symbolizes far more than that which many understand today "to be a church." It represents that which the Lord means by the word "church." In the same way as the lampstand holds the lamps, so a church is meant to hold the testimony of Jesus. When this testimony is held, there will be mountainous problems and difficulties. The powers of darkness will make that a certainty. They will only be overcome, not by our might, nor by our power, but by His Spirit (see Zechariah 4:6). It requires living faith and obedience to go forward with the work in such conditions; God will, however, level the mountains into a plain so that His building work can be completed. It is also in our day a question, in essence, of priorities. They need to be sorted out, if the Lord is going to act for us.

The three vital ministries which we recognized in the vision of Zechariah, are essential for the progression and completion of this work: divinely delegated authority, divinely initiated intercession and worship, and divinely empowered prophetic ministry. God and man are joined together in this work.

There is no way that we can be fully and relevantly related to God's Eternal Purpose without being involved in the building of the house of God. It runs like a golden thread through the whole Bible and ends in the New Jerusalem, which we are told is the holy of holies, the dwelling place of God Himself (see Revelation 21:22). It is the fulfillment of the word:

> in whom [Christ] the whole building, being fitted together, is growing into a holy temple in the Lord . . .
>
> (Ephesians 2:21 NASB)

If we are to inherit, if we are to be involved in the Eternal Purpose of God, then we need to be involved practically in the building work of the Holy Spirit. We need to be wholeheartedly committed to the building of the house of God, to the building up of the body of the Messiah.

One thing have I asked of the Lord

To be committed to the building of God's spiritual house we need the same attitude and spirit as that of the psalmist when he said:

> One thing have I asked of the Lord, that will I seek after;
> That I may dwell in the house of the Lord all the days of my life,
> To behold the beauty of the Lord,
> And to inquire in his temple.
>
> (Psalm 27:4)

One thing is not many things, nor a few things, nor even two things. It is a single-hearted and costly devotion to the Lord.
    In another Psalm, the psalmist declares:

> For the Lord hath chosen Zion; he hath desired it for his habitation. This is my resting-place forever:
> Here will I dwell; for I have desired it.
>
> (Psalm 132:13–14)

This is the attitude and spirit of the child of God who would possess his or her inheritance, who would win the prize, and who would dwell in the house of the Lord forever. It takes a single-hearted and costly devotion:

> Surely I will not come into the tabernacle of my house,
> Nor go up into my bed;
> I will not give sleep to mine eyes,
> Or slumber to mine eyelids;
> Until I find a place for the Lord,
> A tabernacle for the Mighty One of Jacob . . .
> Arise, O Lord, into thy resting place;
> Thou, and the ark of thy strength.
>
> (Psalm 132:3–5, 8)

The picture that we have is of the Presence of the Lord finally coming home to His eternal resting place. It is the holy city, New Jerusalem, the bride of Christ, and the wife of the Lamb.

This attitude and spirit is summed up in the simple but profound words:

> I had rather be a doorkeeper in the house of my God,
> Than to dwell in the tents of wickedness.
>
> (Psalm 84:10)

Chapter 12

THE MYSTERY OF ISRAEL

We now face a question that is both serious and controversial: what is the place of Israel in the Eternal Purpose of God? Does she have a place, or was she a mere means to an end, a stepping stone to something else more important: like the booster rocket of a spacecraft, falling away when the work of launching it was accomplished! If that is our belief, then again we should ask ourselves whether it is the character of the God whom we know, to exploit people for a purpose He has, and then throw them away when that purpose has been accomplished?

It is interesting to note that Israel is not mentioned by name in the first three chapters of Genesis, or in the last three chapters of Revelation. That fact could lead many Christians to believe that Israel was only a stepping-stone to the birth of the Church. Indeed, from what has been expressed so far in this book, many might feel that it is the right conclusion. In fact, it is only in the twelfth chapter of Genesis, and the record of the conversion of Abraham, that Israel comes into view. God promised Abraham that a unique nation would be born of him, and that in him, and through that especial nation, all the families of the earth would be blessed.

It is of the utmost importance to recognize that the sixty-six books of the Bible are all focused on the Messiah, or Christ. They all speak of Him! His person and His work are the key which opens the whole Bible. All the promises of God, and the covenant which He made with Abraham, are centered in the Lord Jesus. In Him and through Him they are all to be realized (see e.g. Genesis 12:7; 13:14–15; 15:18; 17:7–8; cf. Luke 24:44–47; Galatians 3:16; 2 Corinthians 1:20; Romans 15:8). The promises made to Abraham, and the covenant God made with him, are not annulled or cancelled in Christ, but in Him and through Him are all to be fulfilled. Their fulfillment is based on the finished work of the Messiah. In fact every covenant God made with mankind is centered in Christ. Even the Mosaic Covenant, which was conditional, was to act as a schoolmaster to *lead us to the Messiah*, and His work of salvation (see Galatians 3:23–29).

A people that dwell alone

It is a point worth making that from the beginning, when God made the promise to Abraham, it was clearly understood that Israel would be the means through which the knowledge of the salvation of God should come to every family, to every ethnic group and tongue, on this earth. For the fulfillment of that strategy, the Lord commanded His people to be separate from all other nations, to be a unique nation in and through which God would fully reveal Himself: the rite of circumcision, the marriage laws, and the food laws all had this in mind. They enforced and protected that separation and uniqueness. The prophetic words of Balaam, wrung out of him by the Holy Spirit, state the truth simply: "lo, it is a people that dwelleth alone, and shall not be reckoned among the nations" (Numbers 23:9).

However, it was certainly not the mind of God that Israel should be turned in on itself, to become superior and exclusive. The true meaning of the divine calling was to be an agency, a channel, by which the Word of God and the salvation of God would come to all the nations. All the prophets emphasized and underlined this essential calling of Israel, and all of them promised that it would be finally fulfilled.

The Lion of the tribe of Judah, the Root of David

It is significant that when the elder came to John the apostle, he said:

> Weep not; behold, the Lion that is of the tribe of Judah, the Root of David, hath overcome to open the scroll [mg] and the seven seals thereof.
>
> (Revelation 5:5)

He described the little Lamb as "the Lion that is of the tribe of Judah, the Root of David." The little enthroned Lamb is, of course, the Messiah Jesus. His enthronement began with His ascension to the right hand of God, from where He has ruled ever since in the midst of His enemies. He is waiting until the Father has put all those enemies under His feet for the full and complete manifestation of the kingdom in glory! (See Psalm 110:1–2; cf. Acts 2:34–36.) The fact that He is entitled "the Lion of the tribe of Judah, the Root of David" is surely of immensely important significance. Is such a title merely ancient and antique, looking only backwards to Old Testament history, and therefore irrelevant to the present age? Or is it the present title of the Lamb, and therefore totally relevant for today and the future? In my estimation it is clear that the Lord Jesus *is* still the Lion of Judah, the Root of David, as well as the Lamb on the Throne.

The relevance of this truth for the historic point in time that we have reached in this age, is important and meaningful. The Lord Jesus was born the King of the Jews; Herod saw his birth as such a threat to him that in Bethlehem he murdered every baby boy under two years of age; Jesus was acclaimed the king of the Jews throughout the three years of His Messianic ministry; people called Him "Son of David," and on one occasion welcomed Him as king with palm fronds; He died as the King of the Jews, with only that title written and placed over His head; and He was raised as the King of the Jews; the apostle

Peter declared that it was His Messianic Kingship which God vindicated and confirmed when He raised Him from the dead (see Acts 2:36). When Jesus ascended to the right hand of God, it was therefore still as the King of the Jews, the King of Israel, as well as King of Kings and Lord of Lords, Ruler of the kings of the earth, Head of the Church, and Savior of the World. Simply stated, the Lord Jesus is the Lion of Judah, the Root of David, titles which encompass the whole gamut and meaning of Jewish history. It would therefore be unbelievable to think that He has no concern today for the physical "Seed of Abraham," His beloved friend, with whom He entered into such deep covenant relationship. It should be noted that Abraham *never* owned any part of the land which was promised to him in that covenant, except a field for a family burial plot; nor did he ever live in Jerusalem, or have many children, but only Ishmael and Isaac, of which only Isaac was the "son of promise." In other words, the fulfillment of the promises made in that covenant was essentially, apart from the birth of Isaac, more concerned with the future throughout the whole Old Testament period, and through the whole of the New Testament period, and on to this present day!

The return and the triumph of Israel centered in the Lion of Judah

The fact that God has brought back that physical seed of Abraham from the ends of the earth to the Land of Israel, the land He promised to Abraham and his seed *throughout their generations,* is surely not only unique but stunning! (See Genesis 17:3–8.) It must have something to do with the King of Israel at the right hand of God! No other nation has a history such as this: twice exiled from the land promised to them in solemn covenant, and twice restored to it. The first Exile was for seventy years of captivity, fifty years of exile, to a point a thousand miles east of the Promised Land; the second Exile, lasting some 1900 years, was into every part of the globe. The recreated fertility of the land, from desert and wilderness; the partially restored ecology; the restoration of the latter rains; the rebirth of Hebrew as the mother tongue of some four million Israelis, after an absence of 1700 years, as a living contemporary language; the re-establishment of national institutions, such as the parliament, the army, the police, the judicial system; and the rebuilding of towns and cities which have lain in ruin for many centuries, if not millennia: all witness to the incredible relevance and authority of God's prophetic Word, and the faithfulness of God to the covenant He made with the patriarchs. The modern sixty-one years of Israel's history has witnessed nine wars and two intifadas, and more to come! In those sixty-one years, God has watched over Israel as a shepherd watches over his flock (see Jeremiah 31:10). Through all that conflict and battle, Israel has not only survived, she has also triumphed.

There have been many attempts at bringing peace to the Middle East, in particular, over the on-going and thorny problem which exists between Israel and the Arab nations. They have all failed: The United Nations Partition Plan; the Oslo Accords; the Geneva Initiative; the Roadmap to Peace; the Annapolis Conference; all have proved to be mirage and delusion. All these attempts until the present time have ignored the covenant which God made with Abraham concerning the Promised Land, and which was solemnly confirmed to Isaac and to Jacob.

With the original Islamic agenda, and Islamic militants spearheading its fulfillment, there is not the faintest possibility of a lasting peace. Militant and fundamentalist Islam cannot accept the presence of a Jewish state, since, according to the Quran, Allah has finished with them as a state, or as a national community. In all of this there is one factor which is unique: the Lion of Judah, the little Lamb as slain, is enthroned at the right hand of the Father. The fulfillment of the Eternal Purpose of God for the Church and for Israel is therefore secure.

As touching the election, beloved

It is exactly this truth concerning Israel's place in God's Eternal Purpose to which the apostle Paul unequivocally alluded when he said:

> "As touching the gospel, they are enemies for your sake [i.e. the true church], but as touching *the election,* they are beloved for the fathers' sake [i.e. the patriachs], *for the gifts and the calling of God are not repented of"* [i.e. irrevocable].
>
> (Romans 11:28–29, author's emphasis in brackets)

The fact that the inspired Word speaks of divine election, the gifts and the calling of God as being irrevocable, and a hardening in part of Israel, and the same unsaved and partially hardened Israel being saved, means that there is a divine destiny for the Jewish people. It is a significant fact that the Messiah Jesus returns not to the capital cities of great powers, but to Jerusalem, the capital of the recreated State of Israel. The prophet Zechariah makes it clear that it is the literal Jerusalem of which he speaks, when he states: "And his feet shall stand in that day upon the mount of Olives, which is before Jerusalem on the east . . . " (Zechariah 14:4). He gives the precise geographical location! One may well ask why the Lord Jesus, Head of the Church and Savior of the world, returns first to Jerusalem before anything else. Today, in the present climate of world opinion, such a return would not be considered "politically correct." His return to Jerusalem is surely the evidence that the Lord intends to both deliver and save that "partially hardened Israel."
It is also noteworthy that Paul writes:

> For I could wish that I myself were accursed, separated from Christ for the sake of my brethren, my kinsmen according to the flesh, who are Israelites, to whom belongs the adoption as sons, and the glory and the covenants and the giving of the

Law and the temple service and the promises, whose are the fathers, and from whom is the Messiah according to the flesh, who is over all, God blessed forever. Amen.

(Romans 9:3–5 mg NASB)

One wonders who are these "Israelites," if they are not Israelis? We should mark carefully that the Holy Spirit did not say, "to whom belonged," but "to whom belongs." In other words, *it is true of the present time.* The list he mentions is not an insignificant list, but covers the whole Old Testament story and carries us into the present era. All these matters, which Paul mentions, are those unsearchable ric hes into which the true Church has been introduced! We need therefore to recognize *that they still belong to Israel.* Even if none of these other matters were important, then the phrase "from whom is the Messiah according to the flesh" places this whole subject in another dimension. If, as I have stated, the Messiah is still the Lion of Judah, the Root of David, these inspired words of the apostle Paul take on a much deeper significance.

The promise of the redemption and the salvation of the Jewish people

The Lord Jesus said when weeping over Jerusalem:

For I say unto you, Ye shall not see me henceforth, till ye shall say, Blessed is he that cometh in the name of the Lord.

(Matthew 23:39)

It is obvious that before this prediction can be fulfilled, a spiritual "sea change" in attitude, concerning the Lord Jesus, will have taken place in the Jewish people. For them to use these words, which in modern Hebrew mean "Welcome in the Name of the Lord," is evidence of this transformation. Zechariah gives us the clue to it:

> And it shall come to pass in that day, that I will seek to destroy
> all the nations that come against Jerusalem. And I will pour
> upon the house of David, and upon the inhabitants of Jerusa-
> lem, the spirit of grace and supplication; and they shall look
> unto me whom they have pierced; and they shall mourn for
> him, as one mourneth for his only son, and shall be in bitter-
> ness for him, as one that is in bitterness for his first-born.
>
> (Zechariah 12:9–10)

He goes on to say that this will lead to the redemption and the
salvation of Israel (see Zechariah 13:1).

This promise of redemption and salvation for the Jewish people is clearly proclaimed in both the Old Testament as well as
the New. Paul writes:

> I would not, brethren, have you ignorant of this mystery, lest
> ye be wise in your own conceits, that a hardening in part hath
> befallen Israel, until the fulness of the Gentiles be come in; and
> so all Israel shall be saved . . .
>
> (Romans 11:25–26)

The Olive Tree described in Romans 11:17–24 is the Tree in
which are to be found all the saints of the Old Testament era,
and not a small remnant of Jews saved by God in the early
period of the Church. This is the same Olive Tree into which
all saved Gentiles, as wild olive branches, have been ingrafted.
The promise is that the natural branches, the Jews, will be
re-ingrafted when the full number of the Gentiles to be saved has
come in. The Spirit of God, through the apostle Paul, states:

> For if the casting away of them [Jewish people] is the reconcil-
> ing of the world, what shall the receiving of them be, but life
> from the dead?
>
> (Romans 11:15)

This promise of an incredible outburst of resurrection life and power hinges upon the re-ingrafting of the natural branches into their own Olive Tree. The completion by Christ of the building of the Church cannot be accomplished, therefore, without the Jewish people. Those natural branches have to be re-ingrafted for the fulfillment of God's Eternal Purpose.

The New and Eternal Covenant: to the Jew first and also to the Greek

Indeed, this promise of redemption and salvation for the Jewish people is contained in the New and Eternal Covenant of which Jeremiah prophesied when he said:

> But this is the covenant that I will make with the house of Israel after those days, saith the Lord: I will put my law in their inward parts, and in their heart will I write it; and I will be their God, and they shall be my people: and they shall teach no more every man his neighbor, and every man his brother, saying, Know the Lord; for they shall all know me, from the least of them unto the greatest of them, saith the Lord: for I will forgive their iniquity, and their sin will I remember no more.
>
> (Jeremiah 31:33–34)

This is the New and Eternal Covenant which was sealed by nothing less than the blood of the Messiah. It is established on the basis of His finished work at Calvary. The Messiah Jesus said: "This cup is the new covenant in my blood, even that which is poured out for you" (Luke 22:20).

Ezekiel also prophesied of this Covenant when he said:

> And I will sprinkle clean water upon you, and ye shall be clean: from all your filthiness, and from all your idols, will I cleanse you. A new heart also will I give you, and a new spirit will I put

within you; and I will take away the stony heart out of your
flesh, and I will give you a heart of flesh. And I will put my
Spirit within you, and cause you to walk in my statutes, and ye
shall keep mine ordinances, and do them.

(Ezekiel 36:25–27)

The fact is simple! Every Gentile who has been truly saved by
the grace of God has been brought into the New and Eternal
Covenant, which God promised to the Jewish People. The
apostle Paul states this clearly:

> Wherefore remember, that once ye, the Gentiles in the flesh,
> who are called Uncircumcision by that which is called Circum-
> cision, in the flesh, made by hands; that ye were at that time
> separate from Christ, alienated from the commonwealth of
> Israel, and strangers from the covenants of the promise, having
> no hope and without God in the world. But now in Christ Jesus
> ye that once were far off are made nigh in the blood of Christ.
> For he is our peace, who made both one, and brake down the
> middle wall of partition . . .

(Ephesians 2:11–14)

The Lord Jesus referred to this same truth when He said:

> And other sheep I have, which are not of this fold: them also
> I must bring, and they shall hear my voice: and they shall
> become one flock, one shepherd.

(John 10:16)

This is made clear by the words which the apostle Paul used
when he wrote:

> which in other generation was not made known unto the sons
> of men, as it hath now been revealed unto his holy apostles and
> prophets in the Spirit; to wit, that the Gentiles are fellow-heirs,

and fellow-members of the body, and fellow-partakers of the
promise in Christ Jesus through the gospel . . .

(Ephesians 3:5–6)

It is interesting to note the biblical emphasis: the Gentiles are
"fellow-heirs," "fellow-members," and "fellow-partakers"!
Fellows with whom? Fellow-heirs, fellow-members, fellow-
partakers with saved Jews. This salvation, this gospel, was, and
is, to the Jew first, and also to the Greek! As Paul proclaimed:

For I am not ashamed of the gospel: for it is the power of God
unto salvation to every one that believeth; to the Jew first, and
also to the Greek.

(Romans 1:16)

The divine order is important and significant, since God Himself
has observed it. We should not reverse it!

The twenty-seven books and writings of the New Testament
begin "on the other foot" to the foot that the Church has stood
on for the last 1700 years. In other words, the Christian attitude has been that the Jews have been replaced by the Church,
rather than the Church being the Jewish people's *own Olive Tree*.
When the Lord Jesus said: "For salvation is from the Jews," it
was a foundational and essential truth which He underlined. If
we take the tenor of the New Testament and, in particular, this
inspired statement "their own olive tree," we could say that the
Church also is from the Jews. Certainly it was entirely Jewish in
its first decades.

In the Messiah, a new creation and a new man

Those of you who have followed me through these chapters
will have noted that in the Holy City, the New Jerusalem,
the Bride, the Wife of the Lamb, there are inscribed both the
twelve names of the patriarchs and the twelve names of the

apostles. All of them actually Jewish, but joined with all of those redeemed from the nations, and saved by the grace of God. It is the Song of Moses, the bond slave of the Lord, and the Song of the Lamb which all of the redeemed sing. One glorious song of worship and adoration, of triumph and victory (see Exodus 15; cf. Revelation 15). It is a new creation, a new man, and a new heaven and a new earth wherein dwells righteousness. All has been made new by the One who sits on the throne!

It is then no longer a question of being Jewish or Gentile! In the Messiah there is an entirely *new man* and a new creation. The promise of God to Abraham will have been wholly fulfilled when from every tongue, and race, and nation, a redeemed multitude, which no man can number, will have been "saved to sin no more."

When the apostle Paul wrote to the church in Rome, he spoke of the Mystery or Secret of Israel: "For I would not, brethren, have you ignorant of this mystery . . . " (Romans 11:25). It is the birthright of every truly born-again child of God to know the mysteries of God and this one is included! Sadly many Christians are totally blind to it. For them it is hard to understand how people described in those three chapters (Romans 9–11) as blind, cast away, laid aside, lost, fallen, unsaved, disobedient, gain- saying, hardened, and enemies of the gospel are, as concerning the election, beloved, their gifts and their calling irrevocable! Yet it is *the mystery of Israel* and *only* the Holy Spirit can give the necessary illumination and enlightenment. Where there is an enquiring, humble and childlike approach, the Lord gives such understanding!

It is the Lion of Judah, the Root of David, the Lamb of God who has realized and secured the Eternal Purpose of God and who will finally manifest that triumph in glory. Is it any wonder that the whole creation falls prostrate before Him and worships!

Chapter 13

"HE THAT OVERCOMETH SHALL
INHERIT THESE THINGS"

For God's redeemed people, there is no matter that is of greater practical importance than "overcoming." It is another supporting theme directly related to God's Eternal Purpose and runs throughout the Word of God. Everywhere we look in the Bible, under one name or another, we discover it! From Abel, at almost the beginning of history, to the present era, the writer of the Hebrew letter traces all those who overcame by a living and working faith. He wrote:

> And these all, having had witness borne to them through their faith, received not the promise, God having provided some better thing concerning us, that apart from us they should not be made perfect. Therefore let us also, seeing we are compassed about with so great a cloud of witnesses, lay aside every weight, and the sin which doth so easily beset us, and let us run with patience the race that is set before us, looking unto Jesus . . .
>
> (Hebrews 11:39–12:2)

His list of those who overcame is by no means complete. He himself said that time would fail him to mention everyone who overcame in the Old Testament era. He also brought this matter into the New Testament period, even to this day, with the words, "Therefore, let *us also . . .* "

Many children of God misunderstand the subject of overcoming. They think it is only for a few elite servants of God, and not for the normal child of God. The Greek word translated by the English word "overcome" is *nikao*. It means to subdue, to conquer, to overcome, to prevail, or to get the victory. In colloquial terms, it means simply "to come out on top." For most Christians, the thought of being a conqueror is intimidating. They feel it is out of their reach, beyond the range of the normal; for only especial and radical Christians, a kind of "super brand" of God's children! Many years ago, I asked Theodore Austin-Sparks what it meant to be an overcomer, and I have never forgotten the answer. He was silent for a moment, and then he said, "It is to be in the race, and on course, at the end." Simply stated, overcoming means that *by the grace of God and through living faith*, you come out on top, in spite of the existing conditions and trials.

It is therefore of no great surprise to discover that this question of overcoming is emphasized and underlined in the last book of the Bible. To every one of the seven churches, no matter what their condition, good or bad, the risen and glorified Christ, the Head of the Church, places His finger on the essential need to overcome. When we come to the last chapters of the Apocalypse and see the wife of the Lamb, the holy city Jerusalem, we hear the words:

> He that overcometh shall inherit these things; and I will be his God, and he shall be my son.
>
> (Revelation 21:7)

With these words, God clearly states that overcoming is directly related to inheriting; overcoming and inheriting *for eternity* is linked to overcoming *in our lifetime* on earth, through the testing circumstances and difficult situations, and sometimes through extreme trials.

He that overcometh shall inherit these things

What did the Lord mean when He said: "He that overcometh shall inherit these things"? What are "these things"? If we read carefully the record of the vision which God gave to John in Revelation 21 and 22, it becomes clear that it is the city of God, the New Jerusalem, the bride, the wife of the Lamb. Everything else that is stated in that vision is focused on this. God's capital city is at the heart of the kingdom of God, of a vast kingdom encompassing everything; the bride, the wife of the Lamb, is enthroned with the Lamb at the center of that new heaven and new earth, and indeed of everything in that new creation. The whole of those two chapters is related to this matter.

When Moses and the children of Israel sang their song of triumph over the fall of Pharaoh's army, they prophesied concerning God's redeemed people:

> Thou wilt bring them in, and plant them in the mountain of thine inheritance,
> The place, O Lord, which thou hast made for thee to dwell in,
> The sanctuary, O Lord, which thy hands have established. The Lord shall reign forever and ever.
>
> (Exodus 15:17–18)

These words were prophetic firstly of the literal Mount Moriah, and of Jerusalem and the temple. They were also prophetic of the New Jerusalem and the eternal reign of God and of the Lamb. When Moses spoke of "the mountain of thine inheritance," it is clear that the mountain upon which Jerusalem and the temple were built, was a shadow of that which is eternal. Prophetically, Moses was speaking of God's Eternal Purpose.

It is also worth noting that the New Jerusalem, the wife of the Lamb, includes the overcomers from both the Old Testament and the New Testament eras. We find in the holy city both the names of the twelve patriarchs or tribes of Israel and the names of the twelve apostles of the Lamb: all have come to reign eternally with God and His Messiah. This oneness of the saints from both the Old Testament and the New is summed up in the words:

> God having provided some better thing *concerning us, that apart from us* they should not be made perfect. (Hebrews 11:40, author's emphasis)

This is made clear in the apostle John's vision in which he saw those who had overcome the beast, and his image, and the number of his name, singing the Song of Moses, the bond slave of God, and the Song of the Lamb, saying:

> Great and marvellous, are thy works, O Lord God, the almighty; righteous and true are thy ways, thou king of the ages. Who shall not fear, O Lord, and glorify thy name? for thou only art holy; for all the nations shall come and worship before thee; for thy righteous acts have been made manifest.
>
> (Revelation 15:2–4, cf. Exodus 15:1–21)

It is obvious that in some marvelous way these two communities of faith, the Jews and the Christians, parted on the person and work of the Messiah Jesus, will in the end come together as one on the person and on the work of the Messiah. The prophetic words of Moses will then be finally fulfilled!

Heirs of God and joint heirs with the Messiah

The last time in the Bible that God uses the word "overcome" has great significance for us:

He that overcometh shall inherit these things; and I will be his
God, and he shall be my son.

(Revelation 21:7)

He links overcoming with final inheritance. It is interesting to
note that He does not say, "I will be His Father, and he shall be
My child," but "I will be His God, and he shall be My son." We
should not make too much of this point, but a babe or a child
cannot administer a kingdom; a son can! The son was once a
babe, and a child, but has grown up, and has been trained and
educated for that position. The necessity of spiritual growth,
of education, of discipline and training, is once again implied.

There is much in the Bible about this matter of inheritance.
For instance, the apostle Paul states:

and if children, then heirs; heirs of God, and joint heirs with
Christ; if so be that we suffer with him, that we may be also
glorified with him.

(Romans 8:17)

We should note that all those who are truly born of the Spirit
of God, are called "heirs of God" and thus "joint heirs with
Christ." The very use of the word "heir" is related to inheriting
and inheritance. We know that the Messiah was appointed the
heir of all things by God, and that everything was made through
Him and for Him (see Hebrews 1:2; Colossians 1:17). We know
that He is utterly worthy to be the sole heir. The wonder is that
through His saving work we are made joint heirs with Him.
He is bringing many sons to glory (see Hebrews 2:10). When
we truly know ourselves, this is stunning! We should also note
the significant last part of this statement: "if so be that we suffer
with him, that we may be also glorified with him." There is an
"if"! Again, it is referring to the necessity of suffering, or enduring some kind of tough training and discipline.

The apostle Peter in his first letter also speaks of this inheritance when he writes of being "born again to a living hope . . . to obtain an inheritance, which is imperishable and undefiled and will not fade away, reserved in heaven for you" (1 Peter 1:3–4 NASB). It is important to mark the words "born again . . . to obtain an inheritance . . . reserved in heaven." It is clear that this inheritance is heavenly and eternal, even though it has much to do with a new earth. This inheritance is centered on the holy city, the New Jerusalem, on the wife of the Lamb. There may be much else included in the inheritance of the saints in light, but that is the heart of the matter (see Colossians 1:12 NASB). In view of this, one understands how deeply Paul was burdened for the readers of his letter, that they would be granted a spirit of wisdom and revelation in the knowledge of the Lord, to know "what is the hope of his calling: what the riches of the glory of his inheritance in the saints, and what the exceeding greatness of his power to us-ward who believe" (Ephesians 1:18–20). If we are to realize "the hope of our calling" and inherit, we need that "exceeding greatness of His power" in our experience to reach that goal. We should note that our inheritance is in Christ; His inheritance is in the saints. Is not His inheritance focused on the bride, and is not our inheritance focused on the bridegroom?

All that the Father gives Me shall come to Me

In my estimation, you cannot lose your salvation, but you can lose your inheritance. The Lord Jesus Himself spoke on this subject:

> "All that the Father gives Me will come to Me, and the one who comes to Me I will certainly not cast out . . . This is the will of Him who sent Me, that of all that He has given Me I lose nothing, but raise it up on the last day. For this is the will of My Father, that everyone who beholds the Son and believes

> in Him will have eternal life; and I Myself will raise him up on
> the last day."
>
> (John 6:37, 39–40 NASB)

His words are plain, authoritative, and, I think, incontrovertible. They cannot be explained away by John's temperament, or by any other "ifs and buts." Twice He speaks of those that *the Father has given Him*; twice He also speaks of *raising them up on the last day*. This seems to speak of a salvation from eternity to eternity. There are two further important points that we should note: first, "the one who comes to Me *I will certainly not cast out*." The Lord used the word "cast out," not "reject" or "refuse," implying that once a person has truly come to Him, He will never throw him out. The second point the Lord Jesus made was: "this is the will of Him who sent Me, that of *all that He has given Me I lose nothing*." Note the words "I lose nothing." He did not say, "I lose some," or "I lose a few," but, "I lose nothing"! In the light of this, can a person be truly saved and then lost again?

If there were no other such statements in the Word of God, this one statement is sufficient. They are the explicit words of the Lord Jesus Himself. How can the Father give to Him certain individuals, and the Lord Jesus promise to raise them up on the last day, saying "I lose nothing," without their being eternally saved? If we make so much of the human will that a human being can walk out of God's salvation by willing to do so, it makes a mockery of the unambiguously clear statement of the Lord Jesus, "all that the Father gives Me shall come to Me . . ." It implies that God does not know His own mind, that He did not foresee that certain people would *will to be* the Lord's, and then *will not to be* the Lord's!

It seems to me that those *truly* born of God cannot lose their salvation. Many who seem to be saved have not been in the first place genuinely born of God. It was a mental or emotional decision without a genuine act of the Spirit of God. As easily as they came, so easily they fell away. I remember the many young people of my age who seemed to be converted, and who "attended church," and who have for the most part totally fallen away. Today they have no interest whatsoever in Christ.

There are of course apostates and wolves in sheep's clothing. The Lord even called one of the twelve apostles "a son of perdition [destruction or ruin]" and "a devil" (see John 17:12; John 6:70). Peter described him as going "to his own place" (see Acts 1:25). All of these may represent a percentage of those who profess the name of Christ but are not truly His, and certainly not true to Him. In this light we need to remember the solemn injunction:

> Wherefore, brethren, give the more diligence to make your calling and election sure: for if ye do these things, ye shall never stumble: for thus shall be richly supplied unto you the entrance into the eternal kingdom of our Lord and Saviour Jesus Christ.
>
> (2 Peter 1:10–11)

The possibility of losing our inheritance and reward

Most of the scriptures that are quoted as grounds for losing one's salvation, pertain in fact to losing one's inheritance and reward. That is no small or petty loss! The apostle Paul used a graphic illustration when he said:

> For other foundation can no man lay than that which is laid, which is Jesus Christ. But if any man buildeth on the foundation gold, silver, costly stones, wood, hay, stubble; each man's work shall be made manifest: for the day shall declare it, because it is revealed in fire . . . If any man's work shall abide which he built thereon, he shall receive a reward. If any man's

work shall be burned, he shall suffer loss: but he himself shall be saved; yet so as through fire.

(1 Corinthians 3:11–15)

The illustration is vivid! Being saved "so as through fire" is surely drastic; such a person has lost everything but their salvation. They are saved, but saved "by the skin of their teeth."

The emphasis of God's Word on this subject is more positive than it is negative. The primary focus is on running the race and winning the prize; on pressing forward to the fulfillment of God's purpose; on laying hold on that for which we were laid hold on by Christ Jesus; on reaching His goal. Since He has made provision for the poorest and the weakest of His children to win, the Lord puts all the emphasis on winning, not on losing; on reaching the goal rather than on failing. From heaven's point of view, there is no need to fail, since the abounding grace of God, and the exceeding greatness of His power, is for us and available to us. The Lord has an immensely more powerful and loving interest in bringing us to that goal than we have so often to reach that end.

Chapter 14

CHRIST, THE OVERCOMER IN US

The Lord Jesus made the meaning of overcoming plain when He said:

> These things have I spoken unto you, that in me ye may have peace. In the world ye have tribulation: but be of good cheer; I have overcome the world.
>
> (John 16:33)

He never said, "In me you will have tribulation," but, "In me you will have peace." What He plainly stated, was: "In the world you have tribulation." In other words, in the world you will be pressured, be stressed, and be squeezed by circumstances and situations. Such experience is not so strange, since it is said that, "the whole world lieth in the evil one" (1 John 5:19). Indeed, it would be truly strange if God's children did not experience much tribulation! The powers of darkness will always be the agency by which these tribulations will come upon us, whether directly or through the uncrucified flesh in others, or within ourselves! The Lord Jesus then gave us the key: "but be of good cheer; I have overcome the world." Clearly He understood that this question of "overcoming" would intimidate most if not all of His children. Therefore He placed the emphasis on Himself, and not on us: "Be of good cheer; *I* have overcome the world."

How does His overcoming of the world cheer us up? Surely *we* are the ones who need to overcome. The answer is simple: He is the overcomer *in us*! He overcame infinitely more than we will ever have to face; and in us, He is the power that enables us to come out on top, no matter what problems, or obstacles, or difficulties we may face. The apostle Paul states:

> Nay, in all these things we are more than conquerors through him that loved us.
>
> (Romans 8:37)

It is worth noting what the apostle meant by "in all these things." He lists them in the previous sentence: tribulation, anguish, persecution, famine, nakedness, peril, and sword. "These things" are not minor matters! Thus even in the most extreme trials or circumstances, He can be the overcoming power in us. It is *through Him* that we become more than conquerors!

There is a phrase which the apostle Paul uses in his Ephesian letter: "according to the power that worketh in us" (3:20). Christ is *the* overcomer in us by the Holy Spirit. That is the key! By His power within us, He is able to do exceeding abundantly above all that we ask or think (see Ephesians 3:20). By the life and power of the Messiah Jesus in us, we can become overcomers. It is like the buoys that serve as a navigation mark or a warning of dangers at sea. However stormy the waves, however much they crash over the buoy, it always comes out on top in the end!

In the same letter, Paul writes about "the exceeding greatness of his power to us-ward us who believe, according to that working of the strength of his might which he wrought in Christ, when he raised him from the dead . . ." (Ephesians 1:19–20). Is it any wonder therefore that he says: "Howbeit what things were gain to me, these have I counted loss for Christ . . . that I may know him, and the power of his resurrection . . . " (Philippians

3:7, 10). Within that resurrection life of the Messiah is the overcoming power we need.

A living and working faith which overcomes

The apostle John states the same truth in different words:

> For whatsoever is begotten of God overcometh the world: and this is the victory that hath overcome the world, even our faith. And who is he that overcometh the world, but he that believeth that Jesus is the Son of God?
>
> (1 John 5:4–5)

We should note carefully that John wrote: "whatsoever is begotten of God overcometh the world." He did not write "whosoever" but "whatsoever," as if he was underlining the fact that only what is born of God in us can overcome. He then makes the same emphasis that the writer of the Hebrew letter makes. It is a living, working faith in God which enables the child of God to be an overcomer.

Genuine faith never functions when we become "faith conscious" or "faith centered." When we are centered on the smallness of our faith, and the need for it to be increased, we are paralyzed. It is interesting that the little faith we possess then disappears! So much that is written, or preached, on making our faith more powerful, exhorting us to inflate our faith, is human psychology, and not the faith which is the *gift of God*. For faith to function and to move mountains of obstruction and difficulty, we need only a little faith, as tiny as a grain of mustard seed (see Matthew 17:20). It is not the greatness of our faith which removes mountains: God alone can move a mountain. Faith as small as a grain of mustard seed, once activated, joins us to God and the work is done. Such faith is birthed in us when we see the Lord with the eyes of the heart, and hear the Lord with a hearing ear, a spiritual ear. *The source of all living faith is found alone in Jesus*. He is the author and the finisher, or perfecter, of faith (see Hebrews 12:2). It is this truth which John underlines when he says:

> who is he that overcometh the world, but he that believeth that Jesus is the Son of God?

It is a commentary on the words of the Lord Jesus: "Be of good cheer: I have overcome the world." Do you believe that Jesus is the Son of God? Do you believe that He dwells in you by the Holy Spirit? Then trust *the power that works in you*, and you will be an overcomer! The enormous power which created our universe out of nothing, which wrought the resurrection of the Lord Jesus, and which brought you to a New Birth, *is in you!*

The necessity of patience in overcoming

It is interesting to note the exhortation in the letter to the Hebrews: "let us run with patience the race that is set before us" (12:1). The word "patience" in Greek, *hupomone*, adds another dimension to the normal understanding of the English word. Patience is not merely passively putting up with something, or someone (!), but enduring with a positive steadfastness, a refusal to surrender to circumstances or to succumb under trial.

The apostle John speaks of himself as "your brother and partaker with you in tribulation and kingdom and patience which are in Jesus" (Revelation 1:9). It is interesting to note that this steadfast endurance, or patience, or perseverance, is *in* Jesus. He does not write that it is the patience or the steadfast endurance *of* Jesus, although that would be absolutely true of Him. Instead, there is the suggestion, or implication, that it is in Christ *for us*. John actually writes that he is a *partaker* of the patience that is in Jesus. This is a tremendous encouragement to all of us who feel "battle weary," pressured and stressed. The source of our enduring steadfastness, of our perseverance, is in Christ, and we can be partakers of it. The risen Christ said to the church at Philadelphia: "Because thou didst keep the word of my patience, I also will keep thee from the hour of trial . . . " (Revelation 3:10). What does He mean by "the word of my patience," unless He is commending them for fully obeying His Word, with enduring steadfastness and perseverance, with not a shadow of compromise? In a similar vein, the apostle Paul writes: "the Lord direct your hearts into the love of God, and into the patience of Christ" (2 Thessalonians 3:5). We all understand the need for the Lord to direct our hearts into the love of God, but it is interesting that He can direct our hearts into the patience, the steadfast endurance, of the Messiah.

We have the same word used again:

> Therefore, do not throw away your confidence, which has a great reward. For you have need of endurance [patience], so that when you have done the will of God, you may receive the promise.
>
> (Hebrews 10:35–36 NASB)

Carefully note "a great reward" and "receive the promise." James also uses the same word:

> Consider it all joy, my brethren, when you encounter various trials, knowing that the testing of your faith produces endurance [patience]. And let endurance [patience] have its perfect result, that you may be perfect and complete, lacking in nothing.
>
> (James 1:2–4 NASB)

Note that you may be "perfect" (i.e. mature or full grown), "complete," "lacking in nothing."

If you have followed what I have written about the goal of our salvation in previous chapters, you will recognize that the question of patience is an elementary constituent of overcoming, directly related to God's Eternal Purpose. When we are honest with ourselves, the real problem in overcoming is what the writer of the letter to the Hebrews calls "weights," or "encumbrances," and "the sin which so easily besets us," or entangles us. Overcoming is not the absence of such sins and hindrances: every normal saved human being has this struggle. It is how we face the problem that they represent which counts. All runners will know that any unnecessary weight or encumbrance will seriously affect their running; anything that entangles them could slow them down, if it does not put them out of the race. The apostle Paul writes:

> Do you not know that those who run in a race all run, but only one receives the prize? *Run in such a way that you may win.*
> (1 Corinthians 9:24 NASB, author's emphasis)

In all athletics, there is no alternative to discipline. God considers every one of His own children a potential overcomer, and has made available to them all the needed grace and power to endure the discipline, and win the race.

Hearing the voice of the Lord and overcoming

Hearing the voice of the Lord is also an essential factor in overcoming. In every one of the messages which the Lord gave to the seven churches, He emphasized the need to hear what the Spirit was saying: "he that hath an ear, let him hear what the Spirit saith to the churches" (Revelation 2:7, 11, 17, 29 cf. 26; 3:5–6, 12–13, 21–22). He links this hearing of the voice of the Lord with overcoming. In other words, there is no overcoming without hearing and obeying the voice of the Lord. The gravity of this matter needs to sink into our minds and hearts. When the Lord Jesus spoke to the seven churches, He was speaking to the whole Church on earth, in time and in place, and therefore to us.

Throughout the Word of God, there is a strong emphasis upon hearing God. The Lord Jesus said: "seeing they see not, and hearing they hear not, neither do they understand" (Matthew 13:13). This was often a refrain of the prophets: "they have ears, but they hear not" (see e.g. Jeremiah 5:21; Ezekiel 12:2). It was this matter of having ears to hear, but not hearing or understanding, which led to the Fall. Adam and Eve heard the Lord when He said: "In the day that you eat thereof, you shall surely die," but in hearing, they did not hear. Satan said, "You shall not surely die," and Eve in hearing, heard him and believed him.

The Lord Jesus put this matter of hearing very simply:

> My sheep hear my voice, and I know them, and they follow me . . .
>
> (John 10:27)

There is no creature more loveable or, at times, more dumb than a sheep. I have watched shepherds with their sheep for years, and I am amazed how the sheep know the voice of their shepherd. When I have appeared and spoken to the sheep, they have either run away, or stood there and looked at me as if I was the one that was dumb. To the voice of their own shepherd, they would have immediately responded. They knew neither me, nor my voice. The Lord said: "My sheep *hear* My voice." Every true child of God is meant to hear the voice of the Lord.

When a person is truly born of the Spirit, there is activated, within his or her own spirit, an ability to hear God's voice. There is a vast difference between those who read the Word of God and *hear* the voice of God, and those who read the words and do not hear *God's voice*. The Lord Jesus, the Good Shepherd, knows His sheep and He speaks to them; and they hear Him and follow Him.

Unfortunately, there are people who claim to hear God's voice all the time, but it is the voice of their own soul, and sometimes, far more seriously, the voice of demons. They are the bane of any fellowship, a perpetual pain and problem amongst God's people. I have known a few such deluded Christians through-out my lifetime and pray fervently to be delivered from them. However, we should never allow such deceived "nutcases" to divorce *us* from this matter of genuinely hearing the voice of the Lord. It is foundational and essential to the Christian life, to the church of God, and to the work of God. A "hearing ear" is a treasure beyond computation! Without this living and direct relationship between the Lord and those He has saved, there can be no overcoming.

The lesson of the cleansing of the leper

There is a vivid picture of this truth in the cleansing of the leper. Leprosy was always a picture of sin, and the leper a picture of the sinner. In the Law, provision was made for the cleansing of the leper. Firstly, the blood of a lamb was placed on his ear, and then on his thumb, and then on his big toe. After that, oil was placed on his ear, and then on his thumb, and then on his big toe. We have here an incredible picture of salvation: both cleansing from sin and justification, and then the indwelling and empow-ering of the Holy Spirit. Firstly, the atoning blood touches the ear, then the thumb, and then the big toe: the whole person is thus covered. Secondly comes the oil: first on the ear, then on the thumb, and finally on the big toe.

In the order of the cleansing of the leper, we see the *vital importance of hearing*. Both the blood and the oil are first applied to the ear. What is the meaning of this? If God does not have the ear of the cleansed leper, He does not have the man him-self! With his hands, he will do his *own* work; with his feet, he will walk and run in his *own* paths. It is only when God has his ear that his work will be the work God commands, and the paths he walks in, will be the paths God orders (see Leviticus 14:23–29).

Forever a bond slave of the Master

We have another incredibly beautiful picture of true service: if a bond slave wanted to remain with his master forever, provision for such was made in the Law. The master was to take the bond slave to a door, or a gate, and with an awl pierce his ear. Although the Scriptures do not record it, a ring was then placed in his ear. Then he became a bond slave of that master for life. We may well ask what it has to do with his ear. Surely his hands were the most important matter! After all, hands were vitally necessary in the work that a bond slave would do. Should not the Law have made a provision for a ring to be put on his finger? Or, we can argue, even more important than his hands were his feet. After all, they carry the man's hands; in all the work he has to do, his feet are essential. Should not the Law have made a provision for an ankle bracelet to be put on his foot? It is, however, neither his hands nor his feet that the Lord sees as of primary importance, but his ear. What is the meaning of this? It is quite simple. *If the Lord does not have our ear, He does not have us.* We will always be working our work, not His; always running in our own paths, and not the path He has appointed!

Overcoming has much to do with hands and feet; it is directly related to the work we do with our hands, and the paths in which we walk. However, in God's view, the ear is far more important than the hands or the feet. If we do not have a "hearing ear," we are useless to the Lord. We shall always be "doing our own thing." Our Christian life and service will be largely self-manufactured: built out of the wood, hay, and stubble of our self-life. It will be work done *for the Lord*, and not the work *of the Lord*. To hear the voice of the Lord is to be under His authority and lordship. Then it is a question of obeying His commands, walking in His will, and thus becoming co-workers with Him in His work. For this reason, the Lord places His whole emphasis on the ear: it is a primary essential. Without hearing the voice of the Lord, there is no overcoming.

Overcoming by maintaining the quality of first love

One last but vital matter in overcoming is first love. We have already covered this essential factor in what we have written about the bride, the wife of the Lamb. In the end, divine love is the factor that enables us to persevere and win the race. To love the Lord our God with all our heart, with all our soul, and with all our might ensures that we will "come out on top." Divine love can do no other than win.

> "Put me like a seal over your heart,
> Like a seal on your arm.
> For love is as strong as death,
> Jealousy is as severe as Sheol;
> Its flashes are flashes of fire,
> The very flame of the Lord.
> Many waters cannot quench love,
> Nor will rivers overflow it;
> If a man were to give all the riches of his house for love,
> It would be utterly despised."
>
> (Song of Songs 8:6–7 NASB)

This is the kind of love the Lord is seeking. Is it any wonder that the Word of God says: "Love . . . endureth all things. Love never faileth . . . " (1 Corinthians 13:4, 7–8)?

Certainly the quality of the Lord's love for us is beyond question. It is recorded that "having loved his own that were in the world, he loved them to the uttermost" (John 13:1 mg). He loves us with no less a love. When this kind of love fills our beings, we experience His overcoming love. It has, however, a further consequence: that kind of overcoming love enables us to love the unlovable and the unloving. There is no power in the universe like the power of divine love. Our service, our work, the contribution we make, should not be out of duty, or mere conscientiousness, but should be powered by divine love!

In the history of the true Church, we have much evidence of this kind of love. The early Moravian brethren, for example, powerfully manifested it. They became slaves to reach the slaves with the love of God; they contracted leprosy to reach the lepers with the saving power of God. They went to the extremities in this world in order to reach the unloved. It was radical, "all out" devotion and love, easily despised by the lukewarm Christian as "wasted" energy, as unbalanced and overboard! There would have been no John and Charles Wesley, and no great first Evangelical Awakening, which swept hundreds of thousands into the kingdom of God, but for the Moravians. Such love is the kind of love that overcomes. It is a love that gives itself fully, a self-sacrificing love, with no restraints.

It is often much more difficult to love the people with whom we work and live and fellowship than those people who are more distant from us. Some Christians have an inbuilt irritant, abrasive and prickly, which brings out the worst in other believers. They have an uncanny ability to get "under their skin." It is almost as if they cause a spiritual allergic reaction to develop in others! There is no quick and easy answer to this kind of problem. There is, in fact, only one answer, and that is *to die*: in such cases, we have to become "a living sacrifice." For that, we need a baptism of divine love. It is the only way in which we can overcome.

Five fundamental factors in overcoming

In this chapter, we have covered five vital factors in overcoming. All five of them have their source in the Lord Jesus, and in a living experience of Him. It is His power, by the Holy Spirit, that is working in us; it is a living, working, practical faith which has its origin in Him, and joins us to Him; it is the enduring and enabling steadfastness, the persevering patience that is in Him, which by the Holy Spirit is produced in us; it is a hearing ear, a spiritual ability to hear His voice, which He produces in us through a new birth; it is the love of God, shed abroad in our hearts by the Holy Spirit: divine love, faithful and self-sacrificing. These five fundamental factors ensure that we will overcome whatever the tribulations or trials we face.

It is overwhelming to realize that God loves us so much that, in and through the Lord Jesus, He has made available to us everything we would we would ever need to stay the course, win the race, and, as a joint heir with the Messiah, possess the inheritance. Who can ever describe adequately such grace: it is fathomless! It is simply beyond the power of language to define or compute.

Chapter 15

THE HEART OF OVERCOMING

In the previous chapter, we considered five important factors in overcoming, all of which are vital and necessary to it. It is, however, impossible to conclude this book without also considering the words in the Apocalypse which were uttered by a loud voice in heaven:

> Now is come the salvation, and the power, and the kingdom of our God, and the authority of his Christ: for the accuser of our brethren is cast down, who accuseth them before our God day and night. And they overcame him because of the blood of the Lamb, and because of the word of their testimony; and they loved not their life even unto death.
>
> (Revelation 12:10–11)

It is a dramatic picture that is recorded here. We are told that there was war in heaven: Michael the Archangel, and his faithful angels, warring with the dragon, and the fallen angels of darkness and death. The whole atmosphere is one of war, of battle, and of conflict: an enormous confrontation between God and Satan, between Christ and the anti-Christ, between Light and Darkness. We are told that the "great dragon," the old serpent, he who is called the Devil and Satan, the deceiver of the whole world, and the continuous accuser of the redeemed, is cast down out of heaven onto the earth with all his fallen angels (see vv. 7–9). We are also told that he has great wrath, because he knows that he has only a short time left to him.

Whichever interpretation of this vision we adopt, it has serious consequences for the redeemed people of God. Whether we believe that this fiercely intense war and its results is an event predicted for the last era of world history; or whether we believe that it is symbolic, signifying the whole conflict of the ages between God and Satan; or whether we believe it is a combination of these views: there is one matter upon which we can all agree. *The essential and practical truth is that God and His Messiah have won!* The Lamb, the Lion of Judah, and the Root of David, is enthroned at the right hand of God, and with Him, and in Him, the Eternal Purpose of God is secured! For those of us who are saved by the grace of God, there is a further great encouragement. Out of that total victory of Jesus the Messiah, we behold a great company of those who overcame Satan.

They are described in one glorious sentence:

> they overcame him [Satan] because of the blood of the Lamb, and because of the word of their testimony; and they loved not their life even unto death.
>
> (Revelation 12:11)

With these words we have come to the heart of the meaning of overcoming. These are three further foundational factors in overcoming, and they are all contained in this one sentence. They constitute the essence of the matter.

The blood of the Lamb

Let us consider the first aspect: the blood of the Lamb. It is impossible to overcome Satan, the world or the flesh but by the blood of the Lamb. We have already seen that at the heart of a new creation, a new heaven and a new earth, there is enthroned a Lamb as though it had been slain. By the blood of that slain Lamb, this great company of the redeemed have overcome Satan.

The term "the blood of the Lamb" signifies the finished work of Christ; it signifies His atoning death and the salvation He has won for us at Calvary. That is foundational to overcoming. It lies at the root of the five factors we have already considered. No sinner can be saved, or delivered, or indwelt and empowered by the Holy Spirit, apart from the finished work of the Lord Jesus. That work spells our justification in the sight of God. It is the only way that fallen men and women, sinners alienated from God, can be reconciled to Him, and joined to Him in one spirit. The only way in which children of God can face the enemy, is in the righteousness of Christ. *There is no other way!* He alone is our clothing and our armor. We cannot face the powers of darkness and evil apart from the blood of the Lamb, for it spells their complete defeat and our total deliverance. All the power of Satan, all the works of darkness, have been neutralized, nullified, through the death of the Lord Jesus. He has brought their power to zero through His death on the cross. Zero, or nought, is totally definitive: however many times you multiply zero, it will always equal zero! Through that work, satanic strongholds can be cast down: not by our intense emotion, or loud noise, or many words, but by His finished work. Here is the heart of the matter. It is "the Word of God and the testimony of Jesus" in action. As good soldiers of Christ we take our stand in Him, and for Him, and with the word of God as our sword, our weaponry, and our ammunition, we overcome him!

When a child of God has a weak or poor understanding of the finished work of the Lord Jesus, that one is continuously open to enemy assault and activity. *Justification* may be elementary, but it is not kindergarten! It is foundational to the Christian life, to service, to the work of God, and to the building up of the church. It is the key to overcoming. Every stage of a believer's growth is based on the justifying work of the Messiah at

Calvary: from his or her new birth until the entrance to glory. The indwelling of Christ by the Spirit, producing the fruit of the Spirit and the growth of spiritual character, is based on the finished work of the Lord Jesus. Every phase in the walk and service of a servant of God is founded on justification. The empowering of the Holy Spirit, bestowing the gifts of the Holy Spirit and providing the spiritual equipment for the work of the Lord, is founded upon His atoning death, *and on nothing else*. We enjoy, in genuine experience, the power of His resurrection life with all its fruit, its energy, and its fullness on the basis of His death. We can *never* overemphasize this truth, that the Father has given everything in the risen life of Christ, based on His finished work on the cross.

When we believe that it is our zeal, our knowledge, our good and hard work, and our devotion which will attain to a baptism of power and of love, we have opened ourselves already to the accusing work of Satan. At some point, at some stage, the fiery darts of the evil one will find their mark in us. Only the shield of faith in the atoning death and finished work of the Messiah can protect us.

This one short sentence is utter simplicity, but it is profound in its meaning and significance: "they overcame him [Satan] by the blood of the Lamb." Once again we are face to face with the need to see with the eyes of our hearts Christ crucified, and the full extent of His work on Calvary. If we are to reach God's goal, to win the race, to possess our inheritance, it will be by the blood of the Lamb, and nothing else. No one will be part of the holy city, the New Jerusalem, part of the bride, the wife of the Lamb, except through the blood of the Lamb. There can be no overcoming to "inherit these things" apart from His finished work.

Every single person who will be part of that bride and of that city is there because of the work of the Messiah. Everything is founded upon the finished work of that "little Lamb as slaughtered," now enthroned at the right hand of God, in the seat of all

power. Within that one finished work of Christ, everything you
and I require to be saved, to be delivered, and to be changed into
His likeness has already been won for us! All that we require for
the work of God, and all that is required for the building up of
the church and its completion, is given freely through the finished work of Christ. Every one of those described as overcoming Satan, overcame him by the blood of the Lamb. That simple
phrase "the blood of the Lamb," and all it contains in divine
meaning, spells total victory for the children of God.

The word of their testimony

The second part of this sentence is as significant as the first:
"they overcame . . . because of the word of their testimony."
Overcoming is linked in a very real manner to confessing with
our mouth that Jesus is Lord:

> The word is nigh thee, in thy mouth, and in thy heart: that
> is, the word of faith, which we preach: because if thou shalt
> confess with thy mouth Jesus as Lord, and shalt believe in thy
> heart that God raised him from the dead, thou shalt be saved:
> for with the heart man believeth unto righteousness; and with
> the mouth confession is made unto salvation.
>
> (Romans 10:8–10)

We should note here two matters: one outward and one inward,
but both of them essential. We are to confess with our mouth,
and believe in our heart.

It has already been pointed out that this last book of the
Bible refers a number of times to "the Word of God and
the testimony of Jesus." The phrase used here, "the word of
their testimony," is not the same in its meaning, but seems to
borrow something from the former statement. It means the
confession of one's faith and trust in the Lord and in the Word
of God.

It is a remarkable fact that when we genuinely worship the Lord, we are confessing with our mouth spiritual and eternal truth. When we declare *Jesus is Lord*, something happens in the atmosphere! If we say, "May Jesus be Lord," or ask that He will be Lord, it is not the same! When with our mouths we confess and say, "I *am* saved," there is a witness of the Holy Spirit with our spirit that we are children of God. "The word of our testimony" is simply expressing with our mouth the truth as it is in Jesus: it is not *a vague hope* that someday Jesus will be Lord, or that His truth will prevail at some future date, or that His kingdom will be manifested at some future point. The word of our testimony is the confession at the point of time we are in, whatever the circumstances or situations or conditions, that He *is* Lord; that He *is* enthroned; that all power and authority in heaven and on earth *is* vested in His hands; that His kingdom *has* come within us already! The faith that is in our hearts is expressed with our lips. In that moment we overcome Satan. There is nothing he can do, because he knows that we are expressing with our mouths what is in fact the truth and the reality. That is overcoming!

The word of our testimony is the proclamation of the blood of the Lamb, the finished work of the Lord Jesus. It is also the proclamation of His resurrection and His ascension. *When we confess with our mouths we proclaim actual facts!* To put it in a colloquial manner, the word of our testimony has no "ifs and buts and maybes." When we begin to see this important matter, we begin to understand a little more of the function of true worship in the conflict that we are in. That great company of overcomers who prevailed in the battle, gained the victory over Satan and his hosts not only by the blood of the Lamb but by the word of their testimony. It was the confession of their living faith.

Together we are to proclaim that He is risen from the dead, that He is enthroned at God's right hand, that He has won the battle; and therefore the end is secured. It is only a question of time before Christ's present, full and total victory will be

universally manifested on this earth. The powers of darkness
hate such a confession. They will do everything in their power
to compromise, to weaken, and even to extinguish the word
of our testimony. Like some tropical bullfrog, or some kind of
exotic bird, they will inflate themselves in order to intimidate
us; to put fear into us! It is, however, all show! We must learn
"to stand," "to withstand," "and having done all, to stand"! (See
Ephesians 6:11, 13, 14.) It is important at this point to underline
the need to be very careful over the manner in which we confront the powers of darkness. We must never speak disrespect-
fully or crudely to them. Instead we should keep to the positive:
Christ *is* Lord; He is enthroned and all the power of Satan has
been brought to nought by His finished work. Satan and his
legions have no answer to that kind of confession of truth. They
deal in lies and cannot handle the truth. When it comes to the
profession of truth, those dark forces have no weapon against
such a testimony. The simple confession that Jesus is Lord,
overcomes Satan and the powers of darkness, however powerful they may appear to be.

They loved not their life even unto death

The last part of this extraordinary statement is: "and they loved
not their life even unto death." It is interesting to note that this
is not expressed in the same way as the previous two parts of
this sentence. We are told that they overcame Satan because
of the blood of the Lamb and the same word "because" is used
again, because of the word of their testimony. In other words,
these are two vital factors in overcoming the Devil. The last
part of the sentence, "they loved not their life even unto death,"
is put in such a manner as if it underlies the other two aspects
of overcoming.

The Greek word for the English word translated "life" is
psuche, soul or self-life, from which the words "psychology"
and "psychiatry" are derived. It is obvious that this last part of

the statement is an essential aspect of overcoming. The whole problem of the defeat which most of us suffer, is centered in our soul-life. It is "egoistic" life: self-preserving, self-advancing, self-glorifying life; it is the life in which *I* come first, and *I* come last. It is the greatest single cause of the breakdown of the Christian life in most believers, and certainly the reason for the major part of failure in Christian work and service. That uncrucified self-life also lies at the root of most of the breakdown in fellowship, and is the cause of divisions and factions. Amongst believers it unfailingly destroys the life of the church.

The Lord Jesus was uncompromising in His standpoint on this matter. Again and again, He placed His finger on the matter of our self-life. For example:

> And he that doth not take his cross and follow after me, is not worthy of me. He that findeth his *life* shall lose it, and he that loseth his *life* for my sake shall find it.
>
> (Matthew 10:38–39, author's emphasis)

Again:

> Whosoever shall seek to gain his *life* shall lose it: but whosoever shall lose his *life* shall preserve it.
>
> (Luke 17:33, author's emphasis)

Again:

> If any man would come after me, let him deny himself, and take up his cross, and follow me. For whosoever shall save his *life* shall lose it, and whosoever shall lose his *life* for my sake and the gospel's shall save it.
>
> (Mark 8:34–35, author's emphasis)

In all these verses it is the same Greek word *psuche*, soul or self-life, which is translated simply "life." It has a real bearing on our understanding of the statement that "they loved not their life even unto death."

Similarly:

> If any man would be first, he shall be last of all, and servant of all.
>
> (Mark 9:35)

It is impossible for an uncrucified self-life, full of ambition, to be last of all, and the servant of all. Again:

> Ye know that they who are accounted to rule over the Gentiles lord it over them; and their great ones exercise authority over them. But it is not so among you: but whosoever would become great among you, shall be your minister; and whosoever would be first among you, shall be servant [bond slave] of all.
>
> (Mark 10:42–44)

To be a servant is hard enough; to be a bond slave, at the beck and call of a master and all his fellows, is impossible for an uncrucified self-life.

It is patently clear that following the Lord Jesus entails the losing of our self-life, in order to truly find it. The Lord Jesus spoke of denying one's self, or giving up all right to one's self, of taking up the cross, and following Him. This is the missing element in today's preaching of the gospel! There is a whole movement amongst the people of God at present which we could sum up as "the betterment of a Christianized self-life." It is the power of positive thinking. It is not true faith, but "mind over matter." It is another gospel! It is true that the Lord Jesus never spoke of losing one's self-life without also speaking of finding it, or saving it. However, His stark challenge is that there is no way to save or to find one's true self-life, apart from His cross: indeed, no one can follow Him without the cross.

The only way we "find" or "preserve" our self-life is to lose it for His sake! The self-life has to be laid down in a deliberate, cold-blooded act of the will. *There is no alternative.* It is not a question of the betterment of that old self-life. It has been crucified with Christ. *That is the divine verdict!* There is a sentence of death on it: "that we should not trust in ourselves, but in God who raiseth the dead" (2 Corinthians 1:9). When we surrender our self-life, when we "lose it," we rediscover our "self" in Christ! Our self is given back to us, under new management, under His Lordship!

The major reason for defeat in the life of the child of God, or in the work of God, or in the life of the church, is simple: we love our self-life, and will do anything to preserve it. "They loved not their life even unto death." Is it possible to be a true disciple, a witness to the Lord Jesus, and an overcomer, and preserve one's self-life? The simple but stern answer is no! These overcomers had consciously and deliberately let go of their own soul-life, surrendering it to the death of the cross. Every one in that great company who overcame Satan, overcame not only by the blood of the Lamb and the word of their testimony, but had laid down their self-life. When a person has come to that point, they have settled the majority if not all of the issues that have troubled their lives. Such are overcomers.

Satan's main line of attack has always been through the self-life. We witness that in the way he confronted and seduced Eve, and then Adam. Into their unfallen souls was injected a satanic poison which has gone through the bloodstream of the whole human race ever since. World history, the long human story, is the expression of that poison. It is centered in our soul! For this reason, the Lord is so unyielding and uncompromising in the way He confronts us on this matter.

There is no way that we can inherit the full purpose of God, the holy city, the New Jerusalem, the wife of the Lamb, if we are not, by His grace and power alone, overcomers! The sovereign authority and power of God is mercifully thrown behind us to bring us to that end. His abounding and fathomless grace is fully available to every child of God who, with all their failings and weaknesses, wills to walk in the path which leads to glory!

EPILOGUE

Through the pages of this book I have repeatedly emphasized that God's Eternal Purpose is centered in the Lord Jesus alone: without Him there is no divine Eternal Purpose. The Word of God is clear on this matter:

> in him were all things created, in the heavens and upon the earth, things visible and things invisible, whether thrones or dominions, or principalities or powers; all things have been created through him and unto him; and he is before all things, and in him all things consist.
>
> (Colossians 1:16–17, author's emphasis)

We have the same truth expressed in the Ephesian letter:

> making known unto us the mystery of his will, according to his good pleasure which he purposed in him . . . to sum up all things in Christ, the things in the heavens, and the things upon the earth . . . in whom also we were made a heritage . . .
>
> (Ephesians 1:9–11, author's emphasis)

We discover this truth throughout the Bible, and especially in the New Testament. Everything was created through Him, and for Him, and in some way, beyond the understanding of our present intelligence, in Him everything holds together. He is also described by God the Father as the appointed "heir of all things" (Hebrews 1:2).

There is no way, therefore, that a child of God could ever understand God's Eternal Purpose apart from knowing the Lord Jesus. In the final analysis, this matter is reduced to utter simplicity. It is a question of *knowing Him*. Many children of God know about the Lord Jesus, but few know Him deeply and intimately. To know *about* the Lord Jesus and to *know Him* are two different worlds! The Holy Spirit is committed to this task of bringing those who are born of God into an ever-increasing and deeper knowledge of Him. His work is to glorify the Lord Jesus, to take what is His and declare it to us!

The inspired words of the apostle Paul should surely be a cause of continuous amazement and wonder to every true child of God:

> For as many as are led by the Spirit of God, these are sons of God. For ye received not the spirit of bondage again unto fear; but ye received the spirit of adoption, whereby we cry, Abba, Father. The Spirit himself beareth witness with our spirit, that we are children of God: and if children, then heirs; heirs of God, and joint-heirs with Christ; if so be that we suffer with him, that we may also be glorified with him.
>
> (Romans 8:14–17)

Paul, by the Spirit of God, describes an unbelievable relationship. The Spirit of God has been shed abroad in our hearts through a spiritual birth, crying "Abba, Father." It is an amazing description of those who were once hopeless sinners and alienated from God. It is no superficial or shallow relationship which he describes, but one that is incredibly close and intimate. "Abba" is one of the first words that a Hebrew-speaking child learns. It requires no college or university course, no education, not even training. It is a direct and personal relationship, following a spiritual conception and birth. Only the amazing and fathomless grace of God could create such a relationship.

However, Paul goes on to describe the outcome and consequences of such a relationship with God the Father: "if children then heirs: heirs of God, and joint heirs with the Messiah." This further truth is staggering! To be born of God is wonderful enough, but to be described as His heirs and joint heirs with the Lord Jesus is mind-blowing. Here, then, is the practical relevance of God's Eternal Purpose for all those whom He has saved. It is not only the foundational matter of being born again: we have also an inheritance to be possessed. In light of this truth we need to "lay hold on that for which also we were laid hold on by Christ Jesus"; we need to "press on toward the goal unto the prize of the high calling of God in Christ Jesus" (see Philippians 3:12, 14). Therefore, the vital need for each of us is to experience personally and originally the illumination and enlightenment of the Holy Spirit. Without His essential ministry and working, we shall have no understanding of the heart of God or of His Eternal Purpose.

Buried within a short Psalm is a wonderful and profound promise to those who honestly desire to understand the purpose of the Lord:

> The secret of the Lord is for those who fear Him;
> And He will make them know His covenant.
>
> (Psalm 25:14 NASB)

It is an astounding promise. The Lord is prepared to counsel intimately anyone who fears Him. The Hebrew word *sod*, translated by the English word "secret," or "friendship," or "counsel," comes from a root that means "intimate conversation" or "secret converse." Its primary meaning is intimate and confidential speech. It could be translated "intimate counsel," even "intimacy." The idea it conveys is of counsel that is confidential and intimate. Here we have an incredible promise that the

Lord will Himself counsel intimately those who fear Him. "The intimacy of the Lord is for those who hold Him in awe!"

This fear of the Lord, which is the key to experiencing the Lord's intimacy with us, is not cringing or terrified fear, something that is dark and heavy; it is the "awe of the Lord." Sadly the word "awesome" has today virtually become a slang word. Nevertheless, it is the "awesomeness of the Lord," this kind of reverence for Him, which will lead to intimacy with Him. In these present times there is little such fear of the Lord, but often instead a crude and insensitive familiarity and coarseness, which can lead to spiritual corruption, decay, and death. As I have already written, God has birthed a tender, direct and intimate relationship between a saved sinner and Himself. Nevertheless, we need to have always a sensitive awareness of who the Lord is. That kind of attitude leads to wisdom and understanding.

> The fear of the Lord is the beginning of wisdom;
> And the knowledge of the holy one is understanding.
>
> (Proverbs 9:10)

It also maintains a living perennial freshness in the life of the child of God, which, in turn, preserves him or her from satanic traps:

> The fear of the Lord is a fountain of life,
> That one may depart from the snares of death.
>
> (Proverbs 14:27)

The intimate counsel of the Lord is for those who fear Him and He will make them to know His covenant. This covenant is the New and Eternal Covenant, sealed with nothing less than the blood of the Lord Jesus. Into that covenant relationship we have been introduced by the finished work of the Lord Jesus, and God remains absolutely faithful and loyal to it. What then does this promise mean: "he will make them know His covenant"?

The ASV translates it: "he will show them his covenant." Where there is a sensitive awareness of the Lord, where He is held in awe, the Spirit of God will reveal the meaning of that New and Eternal Covenant which He has made with us. We shall progressively understand how complete, and how powerful, is the salvation He has won for us at Calvary; and He will unveil, through His Word, the goal and the aim of that salvation. He will grant us the understanding of His Eternal Purpose which we seek.

APPENDIX

Chart 1 – The Eternal Purpose of God - an Eternal & Spiritual Home

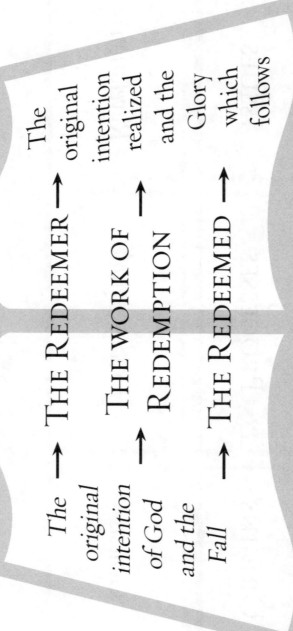

The
original
intention
of God
and the
Fall

→ THE REDEEMER →

THE WORK OF
REDEMPTION

→ THE REDEEMED →

The
original
intention
realized
and the
Glory
which
follows

GEN. 1–3

THE WORD OF GOD
Genesis through Revelation

REV. 20–22

Chart ii – ORIGINS, PROCESSES, ISSUES

ORIGINS	PROCESSES	ISSUES
Genesis	*Exodus – Jude*	*Revelation*

Chart iii – The relation of Genesis 1-3 to Revelation 20-22.

Heaven & Earth GENESIS 2:4	**FALLEN**	New Heaven & Earth REVELATION 21:1
Paradise lost GENESIS 3:24	**MAN**	Paradise regained REVELATION 21:3
Satan enters GENESIS 3:1	**AND HIS**	Satan cast out forever REVELATION 20:10
Earth cursed GENESIS 3:17	**HISTORY**	No more curse REVELATION 22:3
Adam & Eve GENESIS 2:23		A redeemed people REVELATION 21:3, 22:14
A garden GENESIS 2:8		A city REVELATION 21:2
Tree of Life GENESIS 2:9	**THE**	Tree of Life REVELATION 22:2
River of Life GENESIS 2:10	**LAMB**	River of Life REVELATION 22:2
God walking in the midst GENESIS 3:8	**SLAIN**	God dwelling in the midst REVELATION 21:3
Earthly marriage (Man & woman) GENESIS 2:21-25		Heavenly marriage (Lamb & wife of Lamb) REVELATION 21:2
Gold, onyx stone, bdellium GENESIS 2:11, 12		Gold, precious stone, pearl REVELATION 21:18-21
Pain, sorrow & death GENESIS 3:16	**THE**	No more pain, mourning & death REVELATION 21:4
Time ushered in GENESIS 1	**REDEEMED**	Eternity ushered in REVELATION 21
The Spirit brooding GENESIS 1:2		The Spirit and the Bride say 'come' REVELATION 20-22

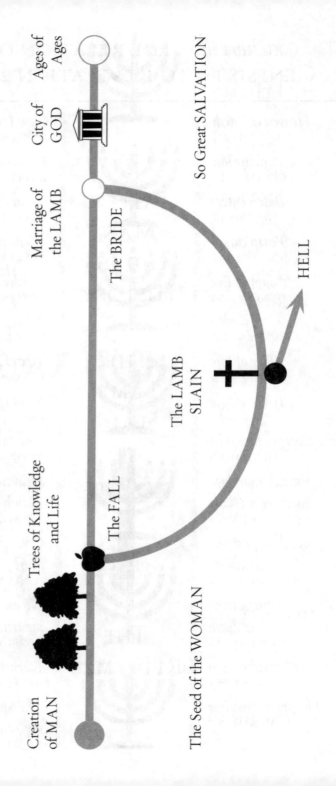

Chart iv – THE ETERNAL PURPOSE OF GOD
CHRIST AND HIS BODY – THE HABITATION OF GOD

The Church at:

EPHESUS

SMYRNA

PERGAMUM

Chart v –
TO HIM
THAT
OVERCOMES

THYATIRA

REVELATION 2:
7, 11, 17, 26-28

REVELATION 3:
5, 6, 12, 13, 21, 22

SARDIS

PHILADELPHIA

LAODICEA

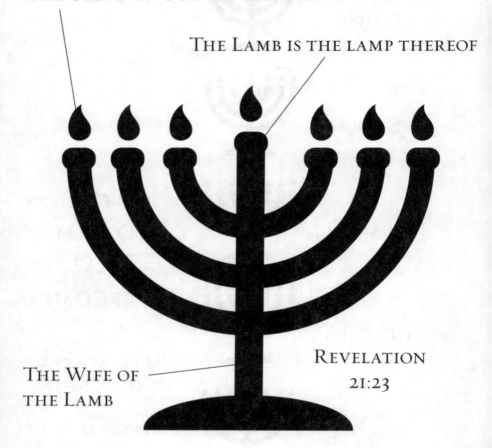

THE GLORY OF GOD DID LIGHTEN IT

THE LAMB IS THE LAMP THEREOF

THE WIFE OF
THE LAMB

REVELATION
21:23

Chart vi – THE CITY OF GOD

He that overcomes shall inherit these things
REVELATION 21:7 (JND)

And they shall reign forever and ever
REVELATION 22:5 (KJV)

ABOUT THE AUTHOR

Lance Lambert is one of the most distinguished Bible scholars and speakers in Israel today and has an itinerant teaching ministry worldwide. Born in 1931 he grew up in Richmond, Surrey in England and came to know the Lord at twelve years of age. He entered the school of African and Oriental studies at London University to prepare for work in China. He studied Classical Chinese, Mandarin, Oriental Philosophy and Far Eastern History, but the revolution closed the door to European missionaries and his entry to China. In the early 1950's he served in the Royal Air Force in Egypt and later founded *Halford House Christian Fellowship* in Richmond. Having discovered his Jewish ancestry Lance became an Israeli citizen in 1980 and now has a home next to the Old City of Jerusalem. His father and many members of his family died in the Holocaust.

Lance is noted for his ecclesiological views, which place him in the tradition of Watchman Nee and T. Austin-Sparks. He produces a widely appreciated quarterly audio recording called the *Middle East Update*, which gives his unique perspective on current events in the Middle East, in the light of God's Word. He has also written numerous books including *The Uniqueness of Israel* and more recently *Jacob I Have Loved*. Lance is presenter of the video production, *Jerusalem, the Covenant City*.

Please visit www.lancelambert.org for more information and to receive the latest Middle East updates.

Also available from Sovereign World

Jacob I Have Loved
The Power of God to Transform a Human Life
Lance Lambert

When God deals with us it is often in deeply mystifying ways. There is no greater example of how God shapes a person than through the remarkable story of Jacob. *Jacob I Have Loved* is far more than a mere biblical overview of the story of Jacob. It is an outstanding illustration of God's desire to utterly transform our fallen inner nature. Despite a twisted, deceiving, sinful heart Jacob nonetheless inherited God's richest blessings and became one of the patriarch's of our faith. Herein lays one of the bible's great mysteries. The amazing truth is that Jacob's name has not been lost in the debris of human history, nor has it been forgotten, as have so many other names. Incredibly, it is forever linked with God. His story is an integral part of the history of divine redemption. This book is about the power of God to transform a human life. Jacob's story is our story.

RRP: £10.99 / ISBN: 9781852404765 / 224 pages
www.sovereignworld.com

We hope you enjoyed reading this Sovereign World book.
For more details of other Sovereign World books
and new releases please see our website:
www.sovereignworld.com

If you would like to help us send a copy of this book
and many other titles to needy pastors in developing
countries, please write for further information
or send your gift to:

Sovereign World Trust
PO Box 777
Tonbridge, Kent TN11 0ZS
United Kingdom

You can also visit www.sovereignworldtrust.com.
The Trust is a registered charity